SELL MORE

MAKE MORE

The Best Sales Systems Ever!

This is what successful people say, do, and when.

Street Smart Entrepreneur Series - Book 2

SELL MORE MAKE MORE - The Best Sales Systems Ever!

Want $1,100 worth of coaching for free?

Go to the last chapter of the book to find out how.

V 2.3

ISBN 9780645212525

Copyright © 2023 Scotty Schindler

All rights reserved. No part of this book may be reproduced in any form or by any electronic or mechanical means, including information storage and retrieval systems, without permission in writing from the author, except by a reviewer who may quote brief passages in a review and must reference the book and author.

This is what successful people say, do, and when.

SELL MORE MAKE MORE

Salespeople are trained, not born! Most people don't set out to become a salesperson. Yet, there are so many people who are front-of-house interacting with clients, meaning they are in sales. Some think they are not, but they are absolutely part of that business's client, sales, and income ecosystem. Many people also become a salesperson because of a job opportunity or business they own. The Problem today is that it's common for technical and product knowledge to get confused as sales training. While product knowledge is essential, it's even more critical to do dedicated sales training on systems so that people know what to say, do, and when.

Here's the reality of business! If there are no sales, there are no clients, no clients means no money, and no money means no interest, then if there's no interest, that means no business.

> *If you're worth it?*
> *And you can prove it!*
> *You'll get paid it!*

The secret is that successful people **make** products people want and **make** money by **making** it happen. They prove that they are worth it!

It's called making money for a reason. Successful people literally make it. And where does all the money come from? A successful financial transaction with buyers. And that's better known as sales!

So when you want to make more money, do more sales training. So well done for reading this book. This is going to pay you back 1,000's of times over.

Now, before I start on the systems, let me qualify how they will help you make more sales and make more money and are the best sales

This is what successful people say, do, and when.

systems ever. I have been a professional salesperson all my life. As a teenager, I walked the streets getting jobs and making pocket money because there was no money if I didn't make my own. And I did go through many different jobs. At 18, I started as an insurance salesman; at 19, I began managing sales teams and have been teaching it ever since. So I have worked on commission-only sales all my life. It's in my DNA.

The true test was when I started a startup company. I created a product that nobody thought they needed and then had to sell the idea and sell it to professional salespeople. That company was called ReNet. It was software for real estate salespeople, so it was 100% sales-based. And in the 18 years of ReNet, I taught many agents how to make $1,000,000+ a year in commissions. So the evidence is real, and that's why I know these street smart systems work and will help you make more sales and make more money; they are your best sales systems ever. If they work for me, and they work for others, they will work for you!

Interestingly, I was one of the few who left school and said they wanted to be a salesperson. Why? Because one of the older guys who surfed at our local beach drove a brand new car (and it was just a Commodore) and was a real estate salesperson. I grew up poor, not homeless, but a single mum and four kids, so I figured that for me to be able to afford a new car like him, I needed to be a real estate salesperson too. So I left school at 17, made fly screens for a year, then at 18, I door-knocked on real estate offices trying to get a job, but nobody would give me a start. But Combined Insurance Company of America did, and that's how my sales career started: selling insurance on commission-only business-to-business, better known as door-to-door. And commission-only door-to-door is a tough job, yet I did that for ten years.

Now I share those lessons with you that are 100% from my personal experience, meaning these systems are not theories. So recognise and relate these systems to yourself, assimilate and take action and use them immediately. The workbook will help you too, and it's available on this book's page at www.system1357.com. Then share your knowledge with others about what you're learning and how they work as you implement

This is what successful people say, do, and when.

them, and finally, practice, practice, and practice. Practice your introductions, presentation and close because perfect practice makes perfect. Find people to practice what to say, do, and when, as it makes all the difference when you need it.

Once you finish this book, I want you to have created your own sales systems. Why? Because many people I meet don't have one, they can't write it down or explain their sales activities as a system. Instead, many respond or react to opportunities, which is normal. But the systems you will create from this book will give you more purpose, be Intentional, and a clear and repeatable action plan of what to say, do, and when. In addition, your systems will avoid potential customers spending money with the competition and help them spend it with you as they become clients.

So make sure you finish this book. Better still, constantly reread this book; every time you do, you will find another way to tune up your systems and make more sales and make more money. Finally, reread it every year as your sales manual for refining and developing your systems, or use it with your team for training and share this book with others who may need it.

And finally, thank you for buying and reading this book, you have made a great decision, and I greatly appreciate it. I'm looking forward to you sending me a photo of you with your copy or even seeing you on social media with your copy. Even better, please tell me what your favourite systems are, along with your success stories. I'd love to hear from you.

It's great to be on your team. Talk soon!

Scotty

About Scotty

Scotty Schindler is a business and sports leader proudly from Sawtell, New South Wales, Australia. Now the retired startup founder and CEO of ReNet, he is recognised as a leading Aussie business identity and keen surfer who has won multiple surfing titles. An overview of Scott's life shows an enviable ability to achieve success in anything he pursues.

At its core, Scotty's career is a story of creativity, hard work and a love of Australian life. As CEO of ReNet, Scott presided over the growth of a startup business that began in 2000 with just one single property listing advertised. On Scott's retirement in 2017, ReNet managed over $1.125 trillion ($1,125,771,059,045) in real estate across Australia and New Zealand by 5,000 real estate offices and some 15,000 real estate salespeople.

In addition to his role as CEO, Scott is also a highly sought-after public speaker, trainer and thought leader within Australia and around the world. A business mentor and sales trainer that can back up advice with proven results in his own life, Scott credits his 'quintessentially Australian' identity as a born optimist and clear-cut straight talker as key to his success in this arena.

Before this present chapter of his life, Scott acquired his business and sales trade during ten years in the insurance industry in the '90s. Other organisations Scotty is actively involved in are the Sawtell Boardriders, Sawtell Business Chamber, Surfing NSW and Fire + Rescue New South Wales. The roles vary, but Scotty's devotion to community is a constant, and so too an unending love of business and surfing that has carved out many, many adventures.

Alongside having represented and won for Australia at the world surfing titles, Scotty also holds multiple surfing championships at all levels of amateur surfing. With an enduring belief that success in business and sport requires dedication to the same qualities, Scotty is also very proud of his work as a coach and trainer of WQS surfers and Aussie surfers in junior development.

This is what successful people say, do, and when.

SELL MORE MAKE MORE - The Best Sales Systems Ever!

When away from his work or sporting commitments, Scotty spends time with his family, and friends and is a proud supporter and sponsor of local sporting groups such as Sawtell Surf Life Saving and Sawtell Scorpions FC.

This is what successful people say, do, and when.

Special Thank You to my Family

To my family, particularly my wife Kazz, for putting up with me over the years and while writing this book, which takes a lot of time. Thank you, but we get to enjoy all the benefits from all the crazy things I do. And my two boys, Jake and Archie, my motivation for System 1357®, it's my burning desire to leave you a family legacy of knowledge, and that's why I keep sharing everything in System 1357® because one day you will want to use some or all of what your dad, grandpa (or whatever I become) used to start, create, grow, and successfully exit a company.

This is for you.

Feedback

If it is OK, please also share your positive book review online. This means way more than you think.

Please write a review on amazon.com or my.system1357.com/books. That would be awesome too.

Thank you!

Scotty

A Photo of You

Please share on social media and tag me in your post with a photo of you and this book. Or send me a picture of you with the book, and I will put your photo on the book's webpage. And when you do, you can even get the chance to win a $1,000 training session (details later in the book).

That's perfect Business Judo® for both of us too!

Thank you!

Scotty

Foreword

Des Bosnic

For centuries people have been looking for a secret to success. What is success? What is the secret?

It can be described in many ways, and success means different things to different people.

Where do you find the secret to success? We live in a world where every answer to any question can be found with the click of a button. The question is, where is the secret hidden? They have said if you want to hide a secret, hide it in the books.

I have been fortunate to manage companies worldwide, from Asia to Europe, then North and Latin America.

What I have discovered is that it doesn't matter where you come from or what nationality, religion, culture or language you speak. Everyone can achieve success provided you have the right systems and a process in place. You will find that this book will give you all the necessary systems that you require to achieve your goals. You simply need to study them and then follow through with action.

We have seen what Scotty has accomplished by developing the best sales systems Ever. Let's learn from his experience and develop the habit of success by using his systems.

Scotty started from humble beginnings with willingness, commitment and determination to improve himself. He has worked hard and long to learn from other successful people and develop systems that everyone can benefit from.

I was fortunate enough to meet Scotty when he was just 18yrs of age. I remember asking who is this kid from a country town, a surfing-looking dude with long blonde hair moving up the management ranks.

This is what successful people say, do, and when.

Scotty always wanted more, did more, and always looked for ways to improve himself.

We now know the secret of Scotty's success. (His Books) Scotty is an established CEO, international public speaker, coach, mentor, entrepreneur, champion surfer, husband, father and international author of numerous books, articles, and systems...

We know that we can adopt his systems and become successful if we are willing to learn.

I was fortunate to be the MC at Scotty's wedding. I have seen his hard work, never-die attitude, and commitment to developing a system that will help him achieve success and, in turn, inspire others to follow in his footsteps.

What has impressed me the most over the years is that he is still the same humble man he was, willing to share the secrets of his success with the world. In this book, Scotty is sharing with us his secret of how we can develop systems to achieve success while having a great balance in life between family and work.

The most impressive thing about Scotty is that over these years, he has managed to be a great father and a wonderful husband while developing great systems and running a very successful company. There is a lot we can learn from him. Scotty has definitely learned how to balance life between hard work and never neglecting his responsibilities as a Husband and a Father. This book will show you how to SELL MORE and MAKE MORE.

Scotty, you are what you preach, you do what you say you are going to do, and you never give up. God bless you.

Des Bosnic

1983 - 2018: Deputy CEO, CHUBB & Executive Vice President, Combined ANZ

2016 - Present: Director at Sphere Insurance Group

This is what successful people say, do, and when.

Contents

SELL MORE MAKE MORE	3
About Scotty	6

Foreword — 9
Des Bosnic — 9

Introduction — 18

SYSTEM 1 — 24

Environment — 24
Your Buying Environment — 24
Buying Conversations. — 26
How Do I Create One? — 27
Honesty — 28
3 Touch Points — 29
Peoples Value! — 32

System 2 — 34

System 1357® — 34
1 = People! — 35
3 = CAN Analysis (Conditions Actions Needs) — 35
5 = 5 Systems of Successful People — 37
7 = The 7 Time Tactics of Successful People — 41
So What's Your Sales System — 45

SYSTEM 3 — 46

3 Ps — 46
P1: People's Personalities — 47
P2: People's Character — 50
P3: People's Behaviour — 51

This is what successful people say, do, and when.

Using the 3 P's	52

SYSTEM 4 — 53

4 Levels of the Human Mind — 53

Examples	55
Two Sides	56
1. Closed Minded	57
2. Open Minds	59
3. Confident Minds	61
4. Belief Minds	62
In Action	63

SYSTEM 5 — 64

The Power of Great Questions — 64

The Golden Rule	65
Socrates Successful Method	68
The 3 Reasons to Ask	69
Keeping it Going	72
Be Rhetorical	72
Questioning a Question	74
Negotiation is Buying	76
Are You Sure?	77
You Get Back to Me	78
Any Questions?	80
The Power in You	81

SYSTEM 6 — 82

So What? — 82

FAB	83
Forget the Features!	84

This is what successful people say, do, and when.

Using Advantages	84
Using Benefits	86
WIIFM (What's in it for me?)	87
No FAB in the Competition	88
Now What?	89

SYSTEM 7 — 91

Zones — 91

Cold Zone	94
Warm Zone	95
Hot Zone	96
The Pull Effect	98
The Magnetic Effect	99
False Positives	100
Retention	101

SYSTEM 8 — 103

Fish Attracting Device (FAD) — 103

Smartest FAD Ever	105
Our FADs	107

SYSTEM 9 — 108

Trojan Horse — 108

World's Best	110
In Our Business	112
Using a Trojan Horse	113

SYSTEM 10 — 114

Using Brochures — 114

Our Objective	117
Give and Take	119

This is what successful people say, do, and when.

Following Up	120

SYSTEM 11 — 123
Involving People — 123

Tell Me, Show Me, Involve Me	124
2 Ears, 1 Mouth	125
Possession is 9/10th of the Law	126
B2B	129
Retention	130
Deliberate Mistakes	131

SYSTEM 12 — 134
Body Language — 134

The Mirror Effect	135
Directing a Prospects Mind	136
Stop Talking	136
Positive Language	137
Belittle the Price	139

SYSTEM 13 — 141
The Cycle — 141

The Sides	142
Beginning and Ending	142
Overselling and Underselling	143
Make Your Own	144

SYSTEM 14 — 145
Introduction — 145

4 Levels of the Human Mind	147
Best Introduction Ever	148
Inference	149

This is what successful people say, do, and when.

Begin With the End in Mind.	150
Your Objective	152
Elevator Pitch	153
Retail Examples.	154

SYSTEM 15 — 156

Presentation — 156

Stop Selling	157
3 Reasons	158
3 Reactions	160
Buyers are Liars!	161
The Competition	163
You're Being Tested	164
One Feature at a Time	165
Emails are NOT Your Presentation	166
How Much Is It?	167
Quiz	169

SYSTEM 16 — 170

Close — 170

Your 3 Closes	171
Was That a Yes Answer	174
Shut Up!	175
Why Hard Close	176
Lock the Sale Away	177
What is Overselling	179
Do you Want Fries With That?	180
When They Negotiate?	181
Buyers Remorse	183
Brochures Won't Close	185

This is what successful people say, do, and when.

This is Not a Close	187
Working Pipeline	187

SYSTEM 17 — 190

Follow Up — 190

4 Levels of the Human Mind	191
Beat Your Competition	192
White Flags	193
Reasons	194
Sow Seeds	195
As Second Impressions	196
It's Not Your Close	198
The Best Follow Up	198
Expect It and Beat Your Competition	199
Don't Bug Them	199
The Best Follow Up Line	201

SYSTEM 18 — 203

Marketing — 203

4 Levels of the Human Mind	204
Marketing is Not Selling	205
4 Gives, Then an Ask	205
As Follow Up	207
Golden Email	208
Business Judo® It.	209

SYSTEM 19 — 211

Leads — 211

4 levels of the Human Mind	213
Prioritise Leads	214

How Much?	217
Generating Leads	218
Cold Calling Sucks	220
Working Your Zones	222
Now What?	**225**

Introduction

If you were to ask 5 master chefs, "What is the best way to make a chocolate cake"? You would probably get 5 different answers. Yet I bet their chocolate cakes would be amazing. I also know that each chef would have a system of making it, their recipe, and any other staff member would have to follow that recipe exactly. Why? Because systems work. Having a recipe or system makes their life easier, and it does in sales too.

Now, let's talk about vinegar, lemons, or limes. I love hot chips (French fries) with vinegar on them. Or freshly grilled fish and chips with vinegar or some squeezed lemon. So good. Or a citrus cocktail with lemon or lime in it. I bet right now your tongue is starting to salivate. For many, the simple mention of vinegar is enough for that to happen. It is for me. And this is why sales systems work. Because, as humans, we are predictable. Every human action has a reaction. And that is why a well-planned sales system works, because, just like talking about vinegar, you can plan actions that achieve desirable reactions.

For example, I was on a road trip recently; this day, it was cool, and it was early (6:20 am), and I felt like a morning coffee, so I drove to a local cafe. I pulled up across the road, and as I got out of my car and started walking towards it, a lovely young lady looked at me and, with a smile, asked, "Are you coming in here"? I thought, wow, how nice. So I said, "Sure are"! Then she continued, "Oh, we don't open for another 10 minutes". And again, she was very nice about it, not nasty at all. So I reacted by returning to my car, going to another cafe instead, and spending my $15 on two coffees and a muffin.

A cafe's system should always be to retain clients and keep them from leaving and spending their money elsewhere, true? Their actions should be about getting potential clients in the door and keeping them comfortable so they enjoy spending as much as possible. You and I agree that their system or actions should not be to push people away.

This is what successful people say, do, and when.

With training on what to say, do, and when, they may have said, "Take a seat, relax, and we'll get the coffee machine started soon".

While $15 that morning may seem insignificant, what if my wife would join me, or I would spend $40 on a big breakfast? And what if their actions sent that $40 away in different circumstances five times a day? That's $200 a day, $1400 a week, or $72,800 a year. Even worse, that $72,800 goes to competition instead, yet the money was on their table and theirs to make. So a better system for retaining clients would make a massive difference to their profit. Now scale it by a business that turns over 10x or 100x that. It's a huge amount of money going to the competition, right?

Now, I know you don't do that. But, even so, let's work on systems that keep that money, better yet, make even more money. After all, if someone has the money and wants our products and services, then why not spend it with us?

> **If you're worth it?**
> **And you can prove it!**
> **You'll get paid it!**

Selling, It's a Trade.

"But Scotty, I am advertising on social media, so why am I not getting more sales"?

"Scotty, I'm talking to lots of people but not making any money!

"Scotty, I have a great product, but I need more sales"?

I hear these all the time. These are the motivation for this book.

So what made ReNet a successful software company? Sales systems and paying clients. My trade was to have positive sales conversations with leads who were happy to buy and keep buying. What I am saying is

This is what successful people say, do, and when.

that people bought and stayed in my environment. And as the CEO of ReNet, people would often ask me, "My son or daughter loves computers. What should they learn"? I always said "sales". Why? Because there are many more educated people out there than me, but they struggle to sell themselves and get paid what they are worth. That's because they don't know the sales trade.

With so much social media marketing, people believe that social media is their sales system. But that's not really selling. Social media is excellent, and people may buy from social media marketing, which is great, but selling is a professional trade. It's a conversation that sells and is more than a sales transaction.

If we think back, years ago, sales knowledge was in every household. When I grew up, we had door-to-door salespeople that sold everything from the encyclopaedia to Tupperware and vacuum cleaners. Everyone knew someone who did selling as a full or part-time job or purchased something from them. Multi-Level Marketing has replaced a lot of door-to-door, but traditional door-to-door meant that sales knowledge was being taught everywhere. Uncle John and Aunt Mary knew their stuff because they were taught sales.

Before the internet, someone entered a retail shop to buy products, meaning store owners had to learn how to sell to that lead and the captive audience immediately. They understood the value of someone walking into their buying environment and serving their customers. People had to learn to sell right then and there. Almost all selling was people-to-people and face-to-face, in a physical and personal environment. But today, this is not the case, which is why I believe sales is a forgotten trade.

True Stories

You will enjoy the sales stories (none are made up) and the experiences I share. They are so that you relate to each of the systems. I am sure you have your own stories and experiences, so combine them with mine, and the systems will relate better to you.

This is what successful people say, do, and when.

I pick on car salespeople in this book because they should know better, and almost all of us have gone into a car dealership before to buy a car. Plus, car salespeople should be regularly trained in sales systems and know how to use them. So they are perfect as very few careers still call themselves salespeople, and car salespeople are one of them. But they seem to have forgotten the trade too.

Here are two true stories about car dealers, which is why I often pick on them. Car salespeople are supposed to be experts and trained professionals in sales, aren't they?

First true story! Lexus of Port Macquarie. In 2015 I wanted to buy my wife a new car. I was shopping around and enquired with this dealer. A couple of emails came back and forward and then stopped. Then six months later, the salesman phoned me and asked if I was still interested in a Lexus. That was a good thing, as at least he had a follow-up system, but he was five months too late! I'd already bought one.

Again, I tried to buy another Lexus in November 2021 from the same dealer and the same salesman, Jarad, believe it or not! But this time, it was different. I wasn't shopping around, and COVID meant demand was high, supply was short and order only, with up to six months of wait times for delivery. So I thought I would buy through them. Nobody does deals to get our business when a market is that hot. We either want it, or they sell it to someone else.

I paid my $1,000 deposit, signed a contract, and scheduled delivery for April 2022. I said perfect, as I was travelling in Tasmania for six weeks at the start of 2022. But during the trip in February, he tried to phone me and emailed me a few times. I was out of range a fair bit and thought I would call him on our way home at the end of February. So I got on the ferry to return, and he emailed me two days ago with an ultimatum. I had to respond in 24 hours, or he would refund my deposit (cancel my order). So I missed his deadline, and he proceeded to cancel my order.

To be clear, the new car was yet to arrive. It was still scheduled to arrive in Australia in April, not February. I would get it if it had arrived early and sat at the dealership. But it wasn't sitting at the dealership waiting for me to pick it up. I paid my deposit and signed the contract. So what was the rush anyway? I was locked in! But not to be. I guess he on-sold my order to someone else already. The market was that hot. Even so, he could have said, "Let's order another one", or did another deal, anything! But no. So now he has missed another sale, again!

> On 23 Feb 2022, at 2:11 pm, Jarad Kreidl Lexus <jaradk@lexusofportmacquarie.com.au> wrote:
>
> Hi Scott,
>
> I haven't heard back from you from multiple previous emails and messages.
> I need to know whether you are still going ahead with your purchase or would you like me to refund your deposit?
>
> Can you please give me an answer within 24hrs.
>
> Thank you
> Regards,
>
> Jarad
> Lexus Of Port Macquarie

So I again phoned some dealers for the same car. The market was less hot. Things were changing fast. And I purchased from another dealer and saved $5,000. And it was now a September/October delivery, but all good. We didn't need a car. It was a hot spot, a like, not a need.

Second true story. In 2015, when I was shopping around, I did decide on a small Mercedes Benz for my wife. I liked it the most out of everything I drove. And I drove many cars so I could choose. Then the Sydney salesman phoned me on a Saturday, and he was perfect with his follow-up. He must have listened to his training. He made me an offer, I counter-offered, and he accepted.

But I am loyal, and I like to buy locally. So I went to my local Mercedes Benz with a printout of the deal and invoice before I put down the $1000 deposit. When I walked into my local dealer, it was my lucky day, the actual owner met me. I showed him my invoice and said that I was buying it. I asked if he could supply one instead of buying one in Sydney. He responded, "That sounds good. Buy it". I think he was calling my bluff.

This is what successful people say, do, and when.

SELL MORE MAKE MORE - The Best Sales Systems Ever!

So I went home, paid the deposit, and purchased the Merc from the other dealer. But then, on Monday, his sales manager phoned me and said, "I am told you are interested in buying a car". I replied, "Sure am, but I was told to buy in Sydney, so I did", and the silence in reply was deafening! Not my fault. I would much rather buy locally. The dealer had a hot buy-now buyer in his hands and then let them go. Can you imagine what the training is like at that dealer? Yet, I am certain car dealers have lots of sales training; it's their profession, but even so, it seems to be a forgotten trade for them too.

I know you don't treat people like some car dealers do. Sometimes it feels like they use a system of treating them mean. It keeps them keen! Doesn't it? It's not to say we are or need to be perfect. But effective systems help us retain more sales and clients when we have a bad or busy day. Your systems help fewer sales and clients fall through the cracks when you are distracted. So your sales systems must be trained, practised, and refined constantly, as in daily.

And regardless of what you trade, tangible, like cars or, as I did, non-tangible, like insurance and software. Or, you could deal in lots of small transactions daily, like coffee, or huge ones over time, like construction. These systems work. It's only the length of your transaction time that is different. Your systems will give you an advantage over your competition, make you an expert and build your buying environment.

Your systems are so buyers don't spend their money with your competition or someone else. Because you know what to say, do, and when.

This is what successful people say, do, and when.

SYSTEM 1

Environment

Most people think a "NO" answer is the worst we get in sales, but it's not. Instead, this is the worst outcome you can get.

> **I purchased from someone else!**

That sucks! And it leaves us asking WHY. Doesn't it?

"I bought your products and services BUT with your competition"!

Why? Why? Why?

Yep, the absolute worst outcome is when someone does buy your products and services BUT doesn't spend their money with you. So they had the money and wanted yours, but they didn't spend their money with you. Instead, they spent it with your competition. And that sucks big time!

Your Buying Environment

Recently I watched a documentary on art. The art expert explained that art is not bought. It's sold! So let me explain the S Myth.

The S Myth (Sales Myth) is that you sell. We don't sell. People buy! And we love buying, don't we? Just like art buyers. So the number one

This is what successful people say, do, and when.

rule of sales is that we don't sell anything. That's a myth. People have to want to buy from us. And when do people buy? People buy when they are in an environment they know, like, and trust, an environment that they feel comfortable buying in.

> **We Don't Sell! People Buy!**

Remember, the art expert said that it was sold, not bought. So how is that different for art being sold, not bought? He is saying the same thing. To sell art, artists have exhibitions, openings, galleries and alike. That's how artists sell their works to buyers, by creating an environment for art buyers to buy in. So when an artist creates a buying environment, there are buyers for their art. See how it works?

Your buying environment is also like a magnet (more on the magnetic effect later in the book); the goal is to attract, sell, and then have clients stick. We want clients to buy and become loyal believing customers. So always look at people as buyers, or better still, clients, and not sales, because we don't actually sell anything. Everything you already know about being positive and selling creates your buying environment. And just like an artist, it's your responsibility to create your selling environment regardless if you do inbound or outbound sales.

So yes, our buying environment is required for both inbound and outbound sales, in other words, when we go out prospecting or when someone comes to us. Although inbound sales to leads are much easier than outbound sales and prospecting for leads, but both need a positive buying environment. The good news is that **All** the systems in this book work concurrently and/or separately to build your buying environment, meaning you can let people buy and stop selling.

This is what successful people say, do, and when.

I say **stop selling**. Hard selling creates friction! Selling sets of a series of actions and reactions. Think of two magnets and bringing the two together. One method sticks them together, and then the other pushes them apart. And creating a positive buying environment is precisely the same. We want to pull leads and clients in rather than push them away. And every system in this book is so you can stop selling and not pitch slap leads while creating that positive pull effect and an environment for people to buy in. And that's how you get sell more and make more money. Remember my cafe experience? They should have pulled me in.

Successful people have systems for creating their sales environment, knowing what to say, do, and when. You can call them habits, techniques, blueprints, or processes, but I prefer systems. First, understand that the most crucial aspect of a sales system is creating an effective environment for people to buy in, just like art. They sell art by creating buying environments. That means they can make more money and buyers don't spend their money with someone else.

Buying Conversations.

My wife loves shopping, and when she buys new clothes, she loves to come home and display them all to me. And when I get a new surfboard, I show her with just as much enthusiasm. And when you buy things, you do the same, don't you? And when people buy a house or car, they get that feeling of achievement and success, and rightly so. It feels great when we buy something we've set goals to achieve, bargain or not. Then when we tell our family and friends what we have purchased, we repeat everything the salesperson told us. Because we all love buying stuff, it's fun!

Yet on the flip side, while we all love to buy, very few people will call themselves a salesperson, even if their career title says so, like real estate salespeople, car salespersons, business leaders, and business owners. To avoid being seen as a sleazy snake oil salesman, some people avoid selling as they are nervous about being labelled. The problem is that they end up with systems like show and hope. They show their products and services and hope someone buys. Even though that does happen,

This is what successful people say, do, and when.

you want more of them to buy, and having a great conversation in a positive environment will lead to more people buying.

If selling scares you, stop it and replace the word 'selling' with 'conversation'. Take the pressure off and only work on constructive and intentional conversations. Remember, people like buying, so let them. These systems avoid the show-and-hope system by intentionally using them to increase our chances that they buy more from you in the environment you create.

How Do I Create One?

"But how do I create an environment, Scotty"?

I get asked this a lot, especially for people who don't have a physical business space, like a retail shop. Physical space or not, our environment is about how comfortable we make people feel. Remember the cafe? It wasn't open yet, but they could have said, "Sit down, relax, and our coffee machine will be on in 10 minutes, and we will get you one then". It's more than a smile. It's how we make people feel.

So all the systems in this book are about creating your buying environment, having comfortable conversations about products and services, and building up know, like and trust so they will want to spend their money with you and not spend it with the competition. So even with a physical environment, such as a retail store, the positive emotional connection people feel during and after the personal interaction creates an excellent buying environment. So the decorations on the wall in a shop or the view at a cafe may look fantastic, but it's much more than decorations. For example, have you ever been to a cafe down in a back street with no views yet welcoming staff who had a relaxed vibe and treated you with respect, and you loved it? That's the environment you purchased. So although the decorations were fantastic, they were more than their decorations on the wall, weren't they?

In business and sales, it's said that we should always be closing. Yet I will not teach anyone to be pushy in their environment! I also won't teach anyone to sell on price or by discounting. So yes, have your

This is what successful people say, do, and when.

unique selling proposition (USP) and your **call to action.** It would be best to create reasons why someone should buy now because if you don't, you let people or sales go. And selling on price is sacrificing profit, and if people like buying, let's create a positive buying environment that allows people to buy at full price while satisfying their needs, meaning we get paid what we are worth.

So what's the reason people will choose to buy from us? They become comfortable with the environment we create. A combination of our approach, personality, aura, etc. It's how they feel before, during and after doing business with us. It's how we interact, involve, transact and close. Our positive environment makes people feel comfortable with us and builds up know, like and trust. And creating our buying environment is arguably the most essential system of them all.

Honesty

Being honest sounds obvious, hey? But some people think that making things up to create a sense of urgency is good. It's not. Dishonest selling is the fastest track to failure. Never tell lies or even little white lies. Always be honest to build up the know, like, and trust. The systems in this book allow you to be honest, build confidence and belief, and do it in a way that creates a positive environment for people to buy now and keep buying in the future.

A quick story for you. I was recently listening to a podcast about criminals. This one story involved those people who phone and rip people off. The police investigator was talking about all the tactics the fraudsters used, and I was thinking, wow, that's precisely the systems I teach. I felt terrible that these systems could end up in the wrong hands. So please use these systems to help you and others succeed, do not use them for evil.

Interestingly, these shonky criminals were organisations, and they used these same sales systems right down to how they trained recruits to follow their systems. So if there is a lesson here, it's that these work. So

This is what successful people say, do, and when.

use them and if you have a team, teach and train these to everybody, and be honest.

3 Touch Points

Every interaction has 3 touchpoints, yep, every single one. First, there's an introduction, then a conversation, a transaction and delivery, followed by a close. It's incredible how many times I have picked up my coffee, and I am the one that says thank you.

In other words, this is what happened in this transaction.

Them: "Who's next"?

Me: "Can I have a coffee, please"?

Them: "That's $5"!

Me: "Thank you".

Sow what they just did with their 3 touch points is this;

TP1: Introduction: "Who's next"?

TP2: Transaction: "That's $5"!

TP3: Close: " ".

It's incredible how often people miss a final touchpoint, a great close! What I mean by a close is not the buying or closing question but the final parting conversation with people. How often do we get served and say "thank you" as we walk away, yet they don't say anything? Sometimes we may receive a throw-away "thank you", and while that's polite, it's not a constructive close as a touchpoint. There's a better system to take advantage of the 3 stages of every transaction and interaction we have with clients. Note that these interactions have nothing to do with a successful sale. In other words, even if someone does not purchase, these 3 touch points happen. Even in our emails, these 3 touch points happen, and they exist even if we don't leverage them, but successful people know what to say, do, and when with each of these 3 touch points.

This is what successful people say, do, and when.

Many people focus on the middle, the transaction, delivery, product, the collecting of money, etc., which is understandable. Most understand the opportunity for a warm welcome. Still, many need a solid follow-through close, that opportunity to have someone transition into our business cycle as a client rather than simply disappearing. Let me explain it more.

For a quick introduction example, I went into a business recently, and there was 3 staff behind the desk. All three were busy, which was fine; one was on the phone, and the other 2 had their heads down, looking serious on their computers. All three looked at me at some point, but all three did not acknowledge me. I felt like I was interrupting their day rather than about to buy from them. That could have been fixed by a simple hand wave, head nod, any acknowledgement, something to say "we see you" and won't be long. That's as simple as a positive introduction interaction needs to be. More effective introductions later in the book, but that's how simple creating our buying environment can be. A better system for them would have been someone acknowledging me as a buyer with something like, "We won't be long" and then a "Thanks for waiting" when we did speak, wouldn't it? Later in the book, there is a whole chapter on introductions. You'll love it.

The closure is the most significant missed opportunity. As a closing example, most people think a "thank you" with a smile is all they need to do, but that's a missed opportunity. Let me explain. Our closing is a massive touchpoint and opportunity for staying open and what's next rather than closure. We have just sealed this deal, so what about the next one? The opportunity in the close is to welcome people back for more. That's when we transfer them from a sale to clients. Yes, say "thank you", now also try things like "see you next time", "let me know how you go", "stay in touch", or "ill keep you updated". See how this creates a positive environment for people to buy in or buy more and stay clients? Yet I bet when you next purchase something, most do not do this to you in any way. Try it. Look for someone who does their closure well, regardless of whether you buy. And then, more importantly, practice finishing your transactions with something unique and

This is what successful people say, do, and when.

meaningful for clients and creating your buying environment and value in the future.

Let's try the $5 coffee again to see the difference.

Intro: "Good morning"?

Me: "Can I have a coffee, please"?

Transaction: "Perfect choice. That's only $5".

Me: "Thanks".

Close: "Enjoy your morning coffee. Thank you, and see you again tomorrow".

Can you see the difference now? See how this touchpoint has a positive closure to our simple $5 transaction. And even though it's very subtle, it's creating the positive buying environment we want. Of course, the larger the transaction, the more we put into it, but it's the systematic approach to finishing a transaction, interaction, and touchpoint, successful or not, that matters.

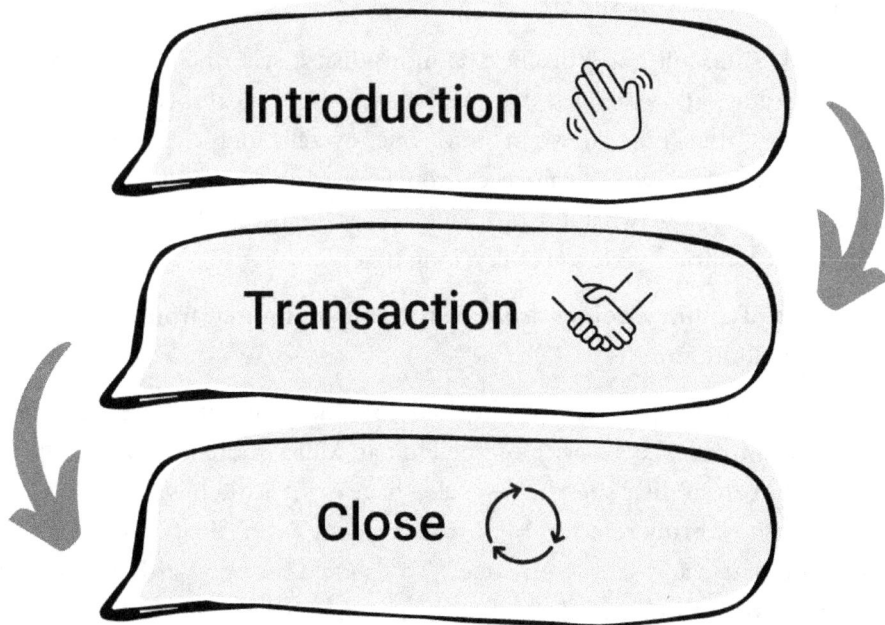

This is what successful people say, do, and when.

Peoples Value!

"I'm not a number. I am a person"!

"I'm not a sale. I am a customer"!

That's how we feel sometimes. Isn't it?

Sales and selling is a conversation that creates clients, not sales, and clients are where the value is. Think of the lifetime value of clients, not sales. And the lifetime value is massive. So they are more than sales. They are clients and customers.

For example, the first 20 clients of ReNet stayed clients all the way to when I fully exited and retired in 2018. Actually, they were clients before ReNet even started in 2002. Over those 18 years, most of those first clients would have spent over $60,000 each, and some spent much more, so over $1,200,000 just on my first 20 clients. So yep, it's interesting that when I started Renet, I already had 20 real estate offices as clients. A few closed down, and a few expanded, but those first 20 clients stayed in my environment the entire journey. As I write this book, I believe many still are.

I talk sales, but good business is more than a sale or a short game. With selling, it's essential that we think about sales as clients and customers and how they fit into our overall long-term business environment. So, yes, I will teach you how to make more sales with these systems, but what I'm teaching you is for your clients to come along on a journey with you over a long time.

A lot of money comes from a little bit of money from a lot of people all the time.

Successful people work on the lifetime value of clients, especially as they go through the 4 Levels of the Human Mind (more on that soon). And apart from their spending, we also have many extra benefits. It was amazing how many referrals I got from my long-term clients. They'd go to conferences and say to someone, "You should use Scott at ReNet for your CRM and website". I didn't even give kickbacks or referral fees or

This is what successful people say, do, and when.

have to do any marketing. My long-term clients would recommend me because we had mutual trust.

The reality is that I'd spent years creating an environment and looking after my customers. I prospected relentlessly and mined for referrals. So lifetime value is more than what they spend with us. It's also all the value the client brings to us. Their value is in revenue, plus referrals and product development too. In other words, clients help us create our environment for them and others to buy.

How much was my marketing budget at ReNet?

Zero! Yep, $0 on marketing campaigns. Not that I recommend $0. It's just how confident I am with sales systems, the systems you are reading about now.

System 2

System 1357®

What's your sales system? If you can't write it down, then you don't have one. And even if you can, implementing System 1357® as part of your sales system makes perfect sense. System 1357® is a compilation of all the systems I used to start a company from zero. That was zero money, zero customers, and zero products, but a system I believed worked. And it does.

You can use System 1357® in its entirety, in addition to anything you are using, and I encourage you to create your version too. Make it your own. Recognise the system, relate it to yourself, assimilate it into your journey, and then take action.

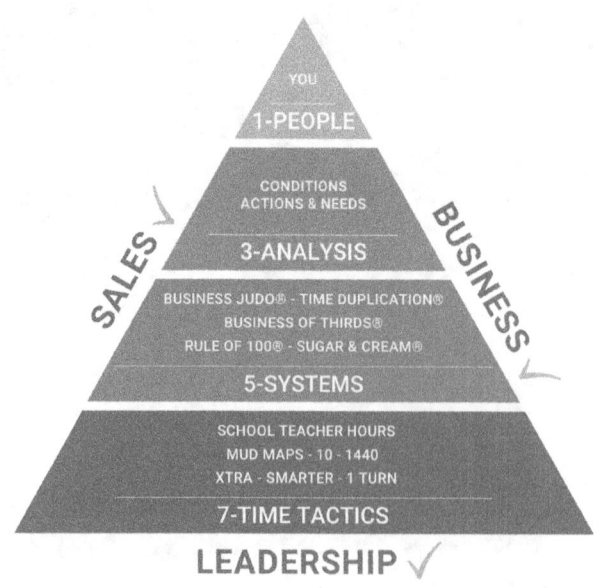

This is what successful people say, do, and when.

System 1357® is comprehensive, and when you read all my books or take my course, you will see this system everywhere.

So let's take a quick and elevated view of System 1357® in sales.

1 = People!

People over everything. We are all in the people business, true?

Many say that I did very well in business, and yes, that's true. And the secret of my success was that I did a great job looking after people: clients and staff. As I see it, we are all in the people business, and they also buy our products and services. So every system in this book is about people first and how to implement them to build meaningful and solid business relationships during and after the sales transaction.

Firstly, let's start with you. You can't fill from an empty cup. What are your goals? What's your why? What's in this for you? Why will you take action? Why will you **make** things happen? Then, and only then, will you do what it takes to achieve your sales goals with the necessary grit, discipline, and determination? Success is not easy, and you need an attitude of "do whatever it takes to get what I want". The sense of urgency combined with an attitude of "if it's to be, it's up to me". Then things happen. Goal setting does not mean things will be easy, but you have a direction you want and become proactive on those goals instead of being reactive to what you are given.

Secondly, when you talk to others about your products and services, it's all about them. Using the word **you** in your sentences is very important as it helps you address the **so what** question in your sales conversations. You will learn more about **so what** later. What are our lead's hot spots, pain, or need? Then, and only then, can we solve it?

People first, people over everything!

3 = CAN Analysis (Conditions Actions Needs)

What's happening, what's doing, what's needed?

This is what successful people say, do, and when.

What's happening, what am I doing, and what do I need?

What's happening, what are they doing, and what do they need?

You can use the exact wording, use the power of great questions (later in the book), or even simply be listening for the answers. But this is not an option. You must know what's happening, what's doing and what's needed before you can succeed.

Conditions; So what's happening? Conditions are easy to see. Anyone can see conditions, but not everyone does something about them, and even fewer try to Business Judo® them and take advantage of them. Conditions are the easiest thing to analyse.

Many conditions go in cycles and generally are not easily changed either, and many are out of our control. Conditions exist, like the weather and seasons, days of the week and months, and even things like elections, economic decisions, school terms, etc. Many things already exist and are out of our control. We can have little effect on them. And just like the Business of Thirds® system, we must learn how to take advantage of them. So it's our responsibility to analyse and maximise them. Will the conditions get better or worse? What happens if we do nothing with the current conditions? Are they fixed, or are they part of a cycle? What will the conditions be like in the future? What do we need to do when these conditions change, and how do we prepare for and take advantage of that change?

Actions; So what are people doing? Are people doing anything, is there an opportunity to fulfil a hot spot, is there a problem or pain point for them, and is there a need we can either fulfil or create? When people have a problem or are in pain, we can solve it and then sell them something.

Actions we do have an effect on. As we go through these systems in the book, you will hear about this effect and our actions and reactions, actions like the magnetic and pull effects, Trojan Horse, and FAD. So listening and understanding people's actions allows us to move with them to achieve their goals.

This is what successful people say, do, and when.

Needs; Then what do people need? Successful salespeople are good at this. They look and listen for needs. And the best thing about needs is that we can either fulfil or create them. We didn't know we needed many things, but someone created a need for us. For example, we all have smartphones now but didn't think we needed them at the turn of the century. But Apple thought about it. Then they created a product while no one else was thinking about it. They did their CAN Analysis on the iPod and turned it into a phone, and that has forever changed our lives.

Looking at needs is something we do every day. As conditions change, people's actions change, and so do their needs. What do people need now and in the future? What products and services do we have to fulfil those needs, or how can we create the need?

5 = 5 Systems of Successful People

Business Judo®. The sport of Judo is the art of maximum results with minimum effort. So one way to describe Business Judo® is the art of leveraging others. Maybe think mental judo. In other words, having a conversation with someone and letting them feel like they're the person that's in control of the situation, yet we're really the ones in control of the environment.

So how do we do that? The way to do that is by using systems like the involvement system and the power of great questions. Engage with them as a person, yet feel like they're in control of the process. Although the reality is that we're in control of the process because we've learned how with these systems. You allow them to have control of their buying environment even though you're in control. And the more they feel in control, the more empowered they are, and then the more likely they will make a positive decision to buy and become a client. Next time you are given a presentation or talk to someone about products and services. If they do more talking than us, they are not letting us get comfortable. They are not letting us be in control. We like to be the one who buys and not be sold to. And that's why we create an environment for people to buy in.

This is what successful people say, do, and when.

The 5 habits of Business Judo® are:

1. PMA: Positive Mental Attitude.

2. Collaboration

3. Leverage

4. Network

5. Win Win Win.

Time Duplication® is the one system every successful person understands! They duplicate themselves, their products and their money.

And there are so many ways we can duplicate our time in sales. How do we say things without having to repeat ourselves all the time? Brochures and websites can be great presentation props. More on that later in the brochure chapter. Depending on the sale, show a short video presentation and leverage it. That's what I did at ReNet when we were selling websites and software. It doesn't have to be ours, as we can use the third person too.

The point is that some things have already been done, and we want to leverage those as much as possible. If we're repeatedly doing something, try to work out ways to present that without having to say or explain it all the time. Let the props do the presentation, and then we use the FAB system (more on that soon) and discuss all the advantages and benefits.

At ReNet, we had a pre-prepared presentation for prospective agents to become clients. That meant we could spend more time romancing the benefits of ReNet while we let them take possession of their software. Time Duplication®, it's essential to look for easier ways to describe our message as we create our buying environment.

Business Of Thirds®, this system made me more money than any other system because ReNet helped agents with their opportunity third!

This system perfectly extends the CAN analysis and conditions, a system for managing the cycles such as the good times and bad times, the success and failures, and the negatives and positives. I made money from this system by showing agents how ReNet helped them manage

This is what successful people say, do, and when.

their cycles and strike rates and where their opportunities were. And it made sense to them instantly.

For example, this is how selling works: a third of people will probably buy, a third will probably never buy, and the other third is an opportunity. The third in the middle are the people who will go either way, depending on our conversation and presentation and what we say, do, and when.

Now, people tend to dwell on the bottom third, those who don't buy, and others relax because of the top third who do buy. Successful people track their strike rates, and they know that it's the middle third where all the success is. Opportunities are in the middle, and they are the people who will go either way, depending on how we engage them and the environment we create for them to buy from us.

Rule of 100™. Very few people have checkpoints for selling, onboarding, and retention. The good news is that you can use the Rule of 100™ system as your checkpoints. That's the first 100 seconds, minutes, hours, days, weeks, and months. These checkpoints are used during the sales process, onboarding and the deliverables for new clients and their retention and lifetime value.

The good news is that with this system. as we get past each checkpoint, we generally get to the next checkpoint. So, if we get past the first hundred seconds, we'll get to the 100 minutes, and if we get past 100 minutes, we'll get to the 100 hours. So, obviously, the bigger the transaction, like a house or car, the longer or more checkpoints come into action as opposed to a quick transaction like buying a coffee.

And the Rule of 100™ starts again once they say yes, during the onboarding or product delivery. When someone says yes, it's imperative now to finish, or close the transaction, congratulate them in the first 100 seconds and welcome them as part of our client base. That makes a big difference to clients and how they feel during and after their buying decision. The Rule of 100™ works in introductions, presentations, and follow-up systems. And it works in countdowns to product releases too.

This is what successful people say, do, and when.

Sugar & Cream®, and when it comes to selling, many people look for cream sales, those cream clients, which is fair enough. If we can get them, then why not? When I started to build websites in 2000, I went to many of the biggest creamiest businesses in town. They were influential, meaning I could Business Judo® it and leverage their names in my presentation, and it worked. I will speak more about inference later in the introduction chapter.

On the other hand, what did I do to start and grow my real estate software company? I did a CAN analysis and decided to look for sugary opportunities. Meaning I didn't go looking for the cream in the marketplace. I went looking for sugary clients in sugary locations.

Let me give a Sugar & Cream® example. I could have gone looking for real estate franchises and gotten bulk sales, as franchises can have 20, 50, or 100+ offices, meaning one big deal in one go, which makes sense. A sale of one-to-many is perfect Time Duplication®. But everyone was trying to get franchises as clients, and they were hard to talk to, so I didn't go prospecting for them. I prospected all the sugary independent offices instead, and the good news was that they wanted to talk to me. It was like selling lollies to kids.

Another example of Sugar & Cream® is the big cities, the big players, the big businesses, the luxury areas, and the cream real estate offices. Well, I never prospected them either! I charged the same amount per office regardless of where or how big a real estate office was. So making money from any office is excellent irrespective of where they were. So I went prospecting in all the regional areas instead, and the regional agents loved me talking to them too. Many appreciated me being there and taking the time to see them. Once again, like selling lollies to kids, sugary clients make things much more manageable.

Where is the sugar in your industry? Where are the sugary clients?

Read the **5 Systems of Successful People** for more. It's a great book too. You will love it!

7 = The 7 Time Tactics of Successful People

Time is the enemy. It's the last thing we think of, yet it's the one thing we all want more of, true? And we all get the same amount of time. Nobody gets any more or less, and nobody can buy more than anyone else. So successful people use tactics to make the most of their time.

Here are 7-time tactics you can use as your tactical response while creating the environment for people to buy in and stay in.

1. School Teacher Hours, this is an excellent tactic as we all went to school, so we all know how that system works. For example, as an analogy, school is Monday to Friday, starts at about 9 am, and finishes at about 3 pm. Each day has a morning break, lunch, and an afternoon break. Days are broken into subjects, like English in the morning, maths in the afternoon, science in economics the next day, and a day for sports too. Finally, the school has terms, in Australia, it's 4 x 10-week terms with two weeks holiday, except summer, which is about six weeks. So it's a system to manage time.

We are not in school anymore, so we need to create our own school teacher hours and lead from the front by scheduling our days, weeks and months. We plan when we are prospecting, following up, or marketing. If we don't schedule our days and time, someone or something else will! So plan and set aside time blocks for emails, phone calls, product development, or whatever we need. Successful people create their own hours, so they are in control. Successful people don't turn up to work and "see what happens today". They already know what their game plan is. (Use the tentative schedules in the workbook to create your own.)

2. Mud Maps, what's that? Well, it's a messy plan, just like someone giving us directions somewhere. They give us their mud map verbally or written; sometimes, it's simple, and sometimes with too much information. We have all had that, haven't we?

In sales, we use this tactic to map clients and share the plan and what they can expect next. For example, when the order is expected, our follow-up with more information, or even what they need to do next.

This is what successful people say, do, and when.

This way, we are not bugging them. They are expecting us. A mud map provides clarity once they become a client about what's next, what they need to do, and what we will do.

Mud maps are a successful tactic because they and we all know what to do or expect. For example, think about booking a restaurant. A great restaurant may also tell us the best place to park if we're early, when happy hour is, and where to sit at the bar. Well, they just gave us their mud map, their tactical response, so we receive a welcoming arrival. Then when we sit down, they involve us again, maybe take an initial order and then tell us they will be back for the main order. And every client needs to be given a mud map, sometimes during but always after the sales transaction, meaning they know, better still, understand what's next. So mud maps are great for your sales systems before, during, and after transactions.

3. 1440, that's how many minutes there are in a day, and we never get them back. So we need to use them wisely. But with that being said, there are 1440 minutes a day, seven days a week, and 52 weeks a year. I believe successful people don't care when they succeed; they will take as much time as it takes. They don't do 38-hour weeks or 9-5, 5 days a week!

I worked on commission when I sold insurance, so the more I worked, the more I got paid. So if there's a chance of a sale, I would chase it. Successful people never chase the clock. Sometimes I would go to events on the weekend because I was guaranteed sales, and if I didn't get sales, I didn't eat. So I used every bit of my 1440 minutes.

Your clients are the same. When is the best time to deal with them? For example, when do they need you to be available in your CAN Analysis? Then fulfil that need, and that's even better when your competition doesn't do this. Make yourself available.

4. Rule of 10 is how we triage time stealers. So the rule of 10 is to ask, "If I do nothing for the next 10 minutes, will the sale get better or worse"? When it comes to selling, there is a lot of truth to "do it now"

This is what successful people say, do, and when.

If someone wants to buy right now, then do it. Why let them go and hope they are there in 10 minutes, hours, days, or weeks?

For example, I tactically won many sales by instantly responding to leads or enquiries. Even if I didn't have the time, I would quickly phone the lead and schedule a proper time. Why? Because I knew the longer the rule of 10 went, the less hot the enquiry and lead became. I will talk more about this later.

Everyone wants our time, don't they? Something can seem urgent to them, and they want an answer right now, but we are in the middle of something. Many use the quadrant of urgent, important, not urgent and not important, but there are two sides, ours and their view of what's urgent. Using the rule of 10 means you can keep things hot for your leads as you combine this rule with the other systems in this book.

5. Smarter goals. SMARTER goals are Specific, Measurable, Achievable, Realistic, and Time-bound, then Evaluate and Reward.

I imagine you are a great goal setter, setting targets and creating an action plan to achieve them. Goal setting combined with a true sense of urgency is the only way to tap into our full potential. It's… I must do this by then, or **the pain of not achieving my goals will be worse.**

The thing is, who we are selling to also has goals. They are trying to achieve something, eliminate pain, or get rewarded for their achievements. It's our job to help them with that, a simple transaction like buying a coffee can still use a micro version of Smarter Goals, but the long-term sales, like houses and cars, we leverage Smarter Goals.

Once again, do a CAN Analysis and set Smarter goals with clients. Again, fulfil their needs, and then mud map them, but this time with an end goal and result, or the delivery of what they have purchased. Setting buying goals is a tactic for us to use as we create an environment for people to buy and become clients. Even if it's a restaurant, like celebrating a birthday or engagement, knowing that goal helps make their night. What are your goals? What are your client's goals?

This is what successful people say, do, and when.

6. Extra Mile. There are two sides to the extra mile club: the over-deliver, under-promise tactic in sales. In other words, always go the extra mile to satisfy clients. But, on the other hand, that could be as simple as a little extra communication during the transaction by going above and beyond while building our buying environment.

The other side of the extra mile is us. Such as doing a little more than everyone else or that is required. I know myself. I had a tactic of doing just one more sales call on the way home every day. When I'd had enough and it was time to go home, I'd look for one more person to talk to. Successful people do just an extra 1% more than the competition. Yep, just 1% more. It was amazing how often that one extra call turned into a sale for me. Committing to maximising my day paid me back more than doing that 1% Extra.

The extra-ordinary results that extraordinary people achieve comes the extra mile. What's your 1% extra?

7. One Turn. This is a surfing tactic, and it's about focusing on the now and the moment. In surfing, I have had many goals to win. But the only thing that matters is the moment or the one turn I am making. The phrase I tell myself is one turn, one wave, one heat at a time. I must focus on the now. Or in tennis, it would be one serve, one game, one set at a time. Or in golf, one swing, one hole, one game at a time.

In sales, this translates to one person, one conversation, and one sale at a time. So when everything else is said and done, ensuring this sale and client happens is the only thing that matters.

In a sales team, during all sales meetings, salespeople will always talk about their sales promises, which is great to have a pipeline. But promises, promises, they don't pay the bills, do they? Only proper sales that turn into clients are what matters.

So the best tactic to seal the deal is to focus on the now and each client while we are with them NOW. They are the only thing that matters, they are in our environment NOW, and they may want to buy, so focus on them right NOW. Don't let them go. Think now or never.

This is what successful people say, do, and when.

So What's Your Sales System

The bottom line is to work your systems, and System 1357® is a perfect system to follow.

1. Put and think people first

3. Do your CAN analysis.

5. Use the 5 Systems of Successful People to work smarter, not harder.

7. Follow the 7 Time Tactics to save time and seal the deal.

Make these your own, modify or use them exactly as they are. By the end of this book, you will be able to write down and document your sales systems. You will know what to say, do, and when.

Even use the tried and proven system of a sales and marketing funnel.

Inside the funnel are your sales systems and warm and hot zones (more on zones later). All your advertising and marketing to get people into your funnel are in the cold zone or outside the funnel. And out the bottom are clients.

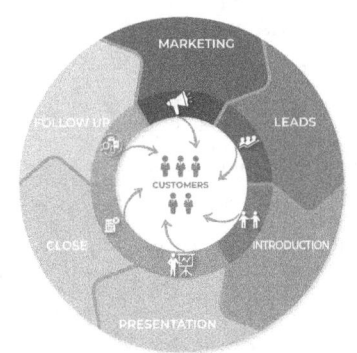

And later in the book, you can also use the business and sales cycle as your system. The point is, it's your system. You can customise any of my systems however you like or follow them exactly as they are. As long as you are winning, then that's the point of these systems.

This is what successful people say, do, and when.

SYSTEM 3

3 Ps

In March 2021, a group of us were mountain bike riding in Derby, Tasmania. We had just completed a few hours of riding in horrendous conditions. Courtney, the organiser, scheduled a stop at a country pub for lunch, they had a wood fire going, and it seemed perfect. A group of guys ordered chicken parmigiana, and suddenly, Courtney said, "My meal is moving". His lunch had maggots over it. Lucky for him, he'd only just started it. Being the nice bloke, he returned his meal and showed the staff. They apologised and offered to refund his money, and he said it was OK. What a top bloke. What would you have done?

Courtney is a pure Labrador of a guy, friendly and a supporter of everyone. So, of course, he'd rather not upset anyone or cause any trouble. But I spent the rest of the day burping up my lunch. Probably nothing wrong with my lunch, but I couldn't get the thought of maggots out of my head. I certainly would have liked a refund for sure.

But we are all different, and the world would be boring if we were all the same. But what makes us different? That's our 3 P's. That's people's personalities, characters, and behaviours. Knowing these helps us understand how we and others react in situations. And knowing these makes a difference in what we say, do, and when.

When buying or selling, we meet people for only a tiny part of their life, and people's moods change, so it's essential not to be too judgemental on first impressions. Like body language (later in the book), we need to look at our interactions as a collective and not judge a book by its cover.

This is what successful people say, do, and when.

Personality and character are part of a person's DNA. How they think or respond is built into people over the years. But behaviour can change very fast, and it can be an instant reaction, and we can definitely have an effect on or are affected by someone's behaviour.

What's the difference between personality, character, and behaviour? Our personality is based on beliefs, while character is how we go about life. Personality and character are the qualities that make us different from others. Behaviour is the way of behaving, the actions or reactions we give to others. Personality is who we are, and behaviour is what we do. When things happen, we don't change who we are, but we react and change how we feel and what we do.

Let me put it this way, do you remember Will Smith at the Oscars? That behaviour was not his usual personality or character, but on that night, it was his behaviour. Who knows what was happening that made him react that way? We will never know, but we know it was a reaction to something someone said.

This is why knowing what to say, do, and when is critical, as our actions will reveal a person's personality and character, which definitely affects their behaviour. And our ability to adapt to who is in our environment matters, especially if we want to have a successful transaction.

P1: People's Personalities

There are many personalities and even more combinations of them. If you have ever studied them, there are many ways to look at them. But I stick to 4, the forgiver, analyser, joker and doer.

Everyone has a primary and secondary personality, along with a touch of all 4, so we have a combination of them all anyway, so let's keep it simple. For example, Will Smith would typically be a fun-loving guy and a Joker, but that night at the Oscars, we saw a different person than we knew. So let's take a quick look at people's personalities in our buying environment. Remember, there are two sides, your personality or ours, and theirs, or our leads and clients' personalities. And we are all different, aren't we?

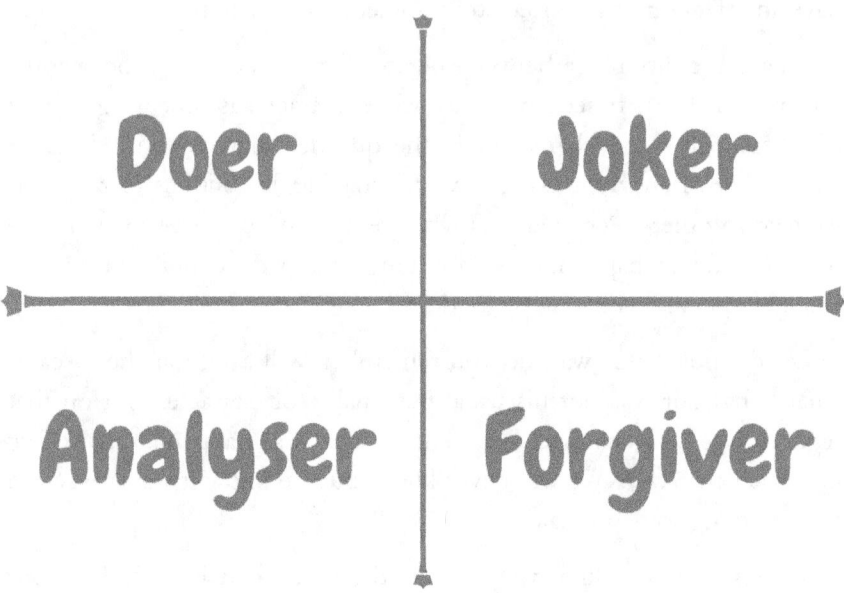

The Forgiver (69%)

Forgivers do not want to make any waves or upset anyone. Instead, they spend time making sure everyone and everything is OK. They are the Labradors of humans, will rarely bite, and are always friendly no matter what. Lucky for us, they are the majority of people.

As buyers, forgivers will never give lousy feedback as they don't want to upset anyone. However, they are harder to read, whereas the other 3 personalities are easier to pick. This is because forgivers always have a second personality trait that gets exposed when pushed. It's also the most dominant second personality trait for the other dominant doers, jokers and analysers. A dominant forgiver and analyser does not want to upset anyone but still wants to know about the numbers. At the same time, A dominant analyser and supporter must know the numbers but won't bother anyone.

Some famous supporters you may know. Nelson Mandela, Hugh Jackman and Tom Hanks.

The Analyser (17%)

The analyser is the slowest buyer and seller of them all. They must know all the figures. If there are no numbers supporting products, then there is no deal. Buying from an analyser is excellent. They're generally trustworthy and compliant; you'll know what you're buying.

As a buyer, the analyser will ask lots of factual questions and need to see the evidence before they know, like, and trust us. Often the analyser becomes a fantastic client as they make informed decisions before they buy. They will not rush in to purchase anything.

The analyser salesperson is often the most knowledgeable, although the other personalities will see them as dull or knowing too much. Often the analyser will seem to be waffling with useless information that they think is important, but it's not! If you're an analyser, keep the figures simple and use the FAB system to support your numbers.

Some famous analysers you may know. Bill Gates, Al Gore and Einstein.

The Joker (11%)

These are fun people, and it's more important that they have a good time than know the numbers.

As a buyer, the jokers want a fun experience more than any other buyer. If our buying environment is not exciting, they struggle to get engaged. They influence and are easily influenced by others and love it when more people are involved. Being left alone is different from how jokers want to be served.

As a salesperson, the jokers are always laughing and are so much fun to buy from. They probably don't know all the numbers and don't seem to care because numbers aren't fun. But jokers will make sure you have a fantastic buying experience. If you're a joker, you're the life of the party,

This is what successful people say, do, and when.

and 89% of other people will enjoy being around you, so make sure you stay focused on why you are there.

Some famous jokers you may know. Richard Branson, Jim Carey and Robin Williams.

The Doer (3%)

The doers are a tough group, and thank goodness for that! They are dominant and direct. Sometimes seem dry or blunt as they want decisions made now and don't care what other people think. You could even think of these as closers or leaders. They know what they know and can't be told otherwise.

If you sell to a doer, you may only get one opportunity. But if you do, the doers stay loyal for a long time. And if you lose them, they will not forgive you. As a buyer, the doers ask, "I want this. How much and how long". And they want a direct answer back from us. So as a seller, be ready to keep up with a doer if you want their business and be direct to them in return.

A doer salesperson is always looking at making quick deals to keep everyone happy. As a seller, they will be assertive and factual in the sales they make, and things happen very fast. If you're a doer, you must slow down for the other 97% of people and let them buy.

Some famous doers you may know. Clint Eastwood, Arnold Schwarzenegger and Judge Judy.

P2: People's Character

Remember, personalities are based on beliefs. At the same time, people have different characteristics or values, and unlike personalities, character definitely changes how people respond to us. Remember, there are two sides. As buyers, we judge a book by its cover. We want to know if the person we buy from is honest, friendly, clean, loyal, trustworthy, etc.

Some characteristics are closely related to personalities, but many operate independently, like trustworthiness and cleanliness. On the other hand, there are some people we don't want in our lives. For example, a dishonest person. They could be the life of the party (a joker) or be highly knowledgable (analyser), but do we want them in our lives? No!

The point is that knowing or understanding people's characters helps us build our buying environment. This is a small list of what people look for when they judge our character.

Honest	Determined
Sense of Humour	Kind
Insightful	Caring
Dependable	Patient
Polite	Loyal
Creative	Tolerant
Organised	Flexible
Authentic	Thoughtful

P3: People's Behaviour

One time I had a hot lead, he said all the right things, and I spent a lot of time with him preparing for their new solution. But then he ghosted me. I couldn't believe he did that after everything I did. What the! It got the better of me, so I phoned, and he answered. I can't remember the opening line, but knowing me, it was something like "How's it all going" to test the water. He said, "Sorry I have not gotten back to you, but my wife passed away. I still want to go ahead, but please give me some time". He didn't ghost me. It's that I was no longer necessary to him. We can all see that would be an expected and acceptable behaviour, can't we?

This is what successful people say, do, and when.

Behaviour is the way of behaving, the actions or reactions we give to others. It is what we do when things happen, we don't change who we are, but we react and change because of what we're feeling or experiencing, affecting our thoughts. So Will Smith was probably a behavioural reaction rather than a personality or character reaction.

The good news is that we can affect behaviour. Remember, people like buying. I know my wife jokes and calls shopping "retail therapy"! When someone buys something, they get an overwhelming feeling of achievement. So we start wearing the new shoes, shirts, or pants we buy for the next few days. Why? They give us satisfaction and make us feel great.

When someone comes into our warm zone, they are all at different levels of behaviour. Some are happy, and some are sad. Some are having a good day, and some are not. Regardless of our behaviour, we want to leave feeling like we have had a great experience. True? We want to feel that we have purchased something to improve our lives.

But what about us? Sometimes it's us that's having an awesome or a bad day. It happens to all of us. Something happens, and we are sometimes celebrating, sad, or even angry. Our behaviour has been triggered as a reaction to something. That's when we have to control our emotions.

So don't judge people on their behaviour. As professional salespeople, it's our responsibility to have a positive effect on others.

Using the 3 P's

The benefit of understanding personality, character, and behaviour in sales is so that we don't judge books by their covers. We are all different in shape and size, including how we think.

When we have an acute understanding of what is happening around us, we can relax a bit more because we understand why, and we can react accordingly.

This is what successful people say, do, and when.

The 3 P's will help you when engaging with your leads, your boss, your teammates, your family, and your friends. But, most of all, it will help you understand who you are, why you say what you do, and when.

SYSTEM 4

4 Levels of the Human Mind

If only we knew what people were thinking!

We have all met people who won't stop talking about something they believe in or hate. The 4 Levels of the Human Mind are the perfect system that quickly shows how people think. Are they believers in the positive or negative? How can we tell, and what do we say and do at each level? What are our and their behaviours like? This is a foundation system you'll love!

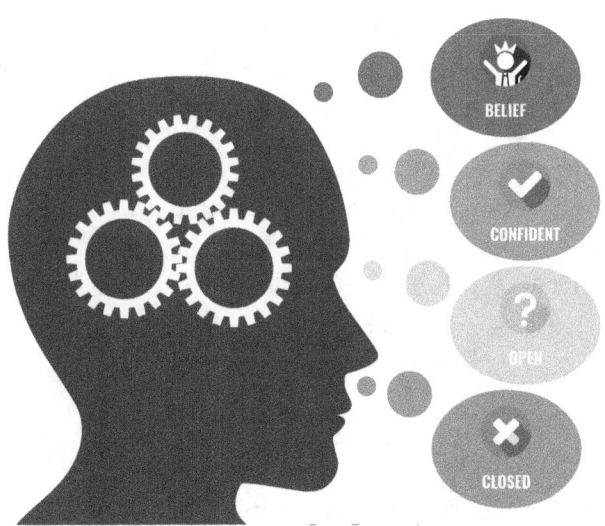

We already know people buy from the environment that we create. Our conversations are so we can assess what someone is thinking. Is there a hot spot, pain, or need? That's why this is one of my favourite systems ever!

I was taught the 4 Levels of the Human Mind when I was 18 when I started working for Combined Insurance during their initial sales course, and now I use it as a foundation for sales, leadership and business. The 4 levels work in every situation. It works from our staff to products, clients, and sales. You name it! The Four Levels of the Human is the perfect system for us to understand the journey that people are going on.

1. Closed
2. Open
3. Confident
4. Belief

Let me explain the 4 levels quickly when it comes to sales. First, a closed mind is very obvious, and we will not be able to get very far with someone who's close-minded. That's like trying to get water to run uphill, so if we can't open their mind, we must let them go.

An open mind is generally where most people are. As a rule of thumb, being open-minded is where most people start. They're asking questions, and they're engaging. They're wondering what colours it comes in, how long it takes, how much it costs over a period of time, and all sorts of open-ended questions. They're engaging and deciding if they'll buy in the environment we have created.

Then we've got the confident people. They probably already know, like and trust our products or services. Let me use a car yard example; Some people go straight to the Ford dealership to buy because they're Ford fans. They've already got confidence in Ford. So it now only depends on which Ford salesperson they will buy from.

The believers will only buy your products and services in your environment. They believe in you so much that they will also recommend you to everyone they meet.

Now think back to my cafe experience at 6:30 am. At first, I was open and even confident in that cafe, but the girl closed me down. So I went elsewhere, grew my confidence in another cafe, and gave my money to their competitor instead. See how quickly it happens?

Examples

Let's look at a sporting example of the 4 levels, say football.

A closed-minded person does not like football.

An open-minded person is neutral, may even watch the big games and is OK that friends either do or don't like or play football.

A confident-minded person plays or has played football and follows it locally, nationally, and at every opportunity. They can and do talk about football all day. When they meet another footballer, that's all they can talk about.

The football believer, we can spot them a mile away. They are fanatics. This is the only game that is as good. So they try to convince us it's the best game, and they try to make us follow their favourite players and teams too. And in extreme cases, if we tell them we don't like football, they instantly don't know, like or trust us in return.

Now reread the above and replace the word football with religion, vegan, fitness, countries, or politics. The 4 Levels of the Human Mind are in play everywhere.

The good news is that anyone can do and use the 4 levels in business. That's having the right conversations with people at the right time. And this book will show you the timing of what to say, do, and when according to where people are on the 4 Levels of the Human Mind in your buying environment.

This is what successful people say, do, and when.

Two Sides

Yes, you may have already noticed that there are two sides to all the systems, and the 4 Levels of the Human Mind is the same. That's our side and their side. What we are thinking and what they are thinking. Remember, System 1357® starts with people, you and them. We are also going through a journey of the 4 levels. We are closed on certain things, yet totally confident or a believer in other things. And when it comes to buying, we don't buy unless we believe that the salesperson has confidence or belief in their products. No one buys from someone who is not, at the least, showing confidence in their products, do they? Or we love to buy from someone who does have confidence and believes in their products, don't we? That's the two sides.

For you, you build your self-confidence and belief by constantly improving, doing sales training over the years and then following the right systems while selling your products and services. The quicker you exude confidence and belief, the better your confidence and belief in your environment will be for your buyers.

For example, the four levels are something we all go through, like when I started door-to-door selling. Now I have been door-to-door or business-to-business selling all my adult life. Most of my day-to-day activities were cold calling in the first 14 years of my career. When I started, I was open-minded but closed that I could make sales. Then after a few years, I progressed to believe in my ability and the products due to lots of training and practice.

When we are outbound or cold calling, 90% of the time, we take someone from a completely closed mind and often very negative, on a journey to open their mind so we can have a sales conversation. Literally, I had to try and open up my presentation folder while they were trying to close me down and get rid of me from their business. And that was not easy! Yet each time I got to do a presentation, I was slowly gaining more and more confidence and belief in the fact that by the end of the presentation, I would have someone confident or

This is what successful people say, do, and when.

believing in what I said so that I could get a sale, or they would become a client. Building up my confidence and belief was a numbers game.

Then when I started teaching sales (I was only 19), I saw the sales trainees go on the exact same journey I went through. Beginning with an open mind that they could sell, but when they would get some rejection, no sales, or both, they would drop down to a closed mind. So my job was to teach them how to sell and build their confidence in their ability to have conversations that lead to sales. It's a tough gig; many can't make cold calls and sell, and many never have the confidence or belief, and I understand why cold calling is tough. And that is why I believe salespeople are trained, not born.

The good news is that the 4 Levels of the Human Mind system used in our outbound door-to-door sales work even better when we have inbound or warm people we can already talk to, and that's how most selling is done today.

So the 4 Levels is a journey that our clients and we go on. And people go through each level systematically, sometimes very fast, and others take months or years. So let's look at them in more detail.

1. Closed Minded

We can tell when someone's closed-minded. They are ghosting us or not responding, and we will not get very far with someone who's closed-minded, are we? So how do we handle closed-minded people when we believe we've got a good product or service for them? If we approach a closed-minded person thinking they are confident or believing, and we talk about price, our timing would be out. Or we'd be overselling, which will only worsen the situation, more on handling price later in the book. We know ourselves, we're window shopping, and someone tries to engage, and we're not even remotely interested. Our body language is to ghost or walk away.

Think about all the spam emails or direct messages we receive. How many are trying to open our minds? But instead, most are 'spray and pray" emails with offers. And what do we do? Delete! Delete! Delete!

This is what successful people say, do, and when.

So what do we do when we have a close-minded person? The good news is that we only need to get them to the open level. If we want their business, then all we're trying to do is open them or warm them up. We create interest, have a conversation, and create a bit of understanding. We are here to listen and open their minds to opportunities or possibilities. Like those stands in a shopping mall, where someone tries to grab our attention with a free sample, they are trying to engage and open our minds to a conversation. How often have we ghosted them or said "no thanks" as we kept walking, trying to avoid eye contact? I bet you do this all the time too. Because you are closed-minded, they are looking for an opening and conversation. See how they use it?

So closed-minded is the easiest level to understand, and it's also the easiest one to handle. When we've got a close-minded person, we can relax a bit more, and there is no need to be offended or lose sleep over them. And if we want their business, we are only trying to open their minds and not sell them anything, well, not yet.

But let's say we are prospecting, and we know we've got something perfect for a potential client, and we're trying to email and phone them. Then all we need do is start a conversation, not sell. So what can we do? How do we open them up? We can compliment them when we see something and communicate it to them. Also, we can find some valuable information to share with them. There's an old saying; **Four gives and then an ask.** Find things that slowly take them to the next level. In other words, just a little bit more to open their mind. Little by little, bit by bit, opening their minds and building know like and trust. Think about prospecting like dating when you were single.

If we go in too fast trying to make sales appointments for this Friday and emailing pitch slaps and brochures so we can sell to them, and they say "no", we're buggered! So now they're even more closed. That's why I spend a lot of time later in the book on the power of great questions. Because we need to lead in such a way that says things like, "I'd like to share something with you", "I'd like to tell you something that will help you", or "I'd like to have a conversation about what other people are using" all in a friendly open-minded tone. Not a sales presentation way,

This is what successful people say, do, and when.

but a warm, open-minded conversation. And remember that a conversation with a close-minded person, someone who's never met us before, needs to be done carefully. Some say we never get a second chance at a good first impression, but in sales, we can when we persist in the right way, and these systems are the right way.

Take little steps and build confidence, so they will want to talk to us. That's the first level. Opening a closed mind takes time. Some people will permanently be closed, and others will open up in seconds, minutes, hours, days or even weeks. The good news is that when you read about the introduction systems later, I will give some unreal systems that open people's minds fast, and you'll love them!

2. Open Minds

An open-mind assumption is the best when it comes to sales. In other words, we don't become overconfident in believing that a person's ready to buy now. Buying can only happen once confidence has been created. So the safest option is to assume everyone has an open mind, which is also the best level to start any conversation. Even if they ask buying questions like, "How much is it"? Think that they are saying, "I am open to more information".

So, how do we know they're open-minded? Because they ask questions, they're engaging and finding out more information. They're playing with our products or services, they've walked into our shop, whatever it is. These are great signs that the person is open to buying. For example, once I walked into a car dealer with my surfboard, I wanted to ensure it fitted into the car. What level was I on? Yet nobody served me.

So what do we do when we recognise someone is open-minded?

This is someone who wants our knowledge, and this is when building our buying environment starts. They have permitted us to have an open conversation with them. We are not doing any closing (yet). We're simply having a constructive, open conversation about our products and services. Assume everyone, regardless of the questions they ask or how

This is what successful people say, do, and when.

confident they look. They are having an open conversation to find out more information. Some people will ask, "Can I take the red one"? And that's OK because that's how this system works, as people often build up confidence in you and your products quickly and then buy.

Treat people as open-minded because the worst thing we can do is over or under-estimate where people are. Let me give a real example, I might be interested in buying a 4WD, I walk into the car yard to get more information, and then nobody comes out and serves me. I would go closed-minded. On the other hand, I get served, but they try to convince me to buy a car when I am interested in a 4WD. In other words, the conversation between the car salesperson and I determines if I go from open to closed or open to confident. I could be enthusiastic about buying, but if they start overselling or underselling, they can lose me as a client. And that's precisely what happened when I walked in with my surfboard to buy a 4WD ute. Here I was, waving a big white buying flag around, but after 20 minutes, nobody served me, so I left. Not being recognised or acknowledged does not mean I am not going to buy the 4WD. It just means that I am going to buy from someone else. And that's exactly what I did!

So there are the buyer's 4 Levels of the Human Mind on the product or services (the 4WD) and the salespersons. And that's what this book is about, building the environment and people's confidence in our products and in us as the salesperson. So if I'm presenting to someone open-minded about my product but becomes close-minded about me, where will they go? Correct, they still buy the product, but buy it from someone else, not me. Let's avoid that!

So the safest level is always to assume people are at the open level. The quickest way to turn someone from open to closed is by asking lousy questions. So use the power of great questions(later in the book). We are friendly, use open and active listening and have a genuine understanding. We are listening to who they are and what they want. The open mind is the safest level until we get enough evidence that we have taken someone from the open to the confident level of the human mind.

This is what successful people say, do, and when.

3. Confident Minds

The confident level of the human mind is the first level that successful sales transactions happen. To what degree are they confident? Only time can tell. As mentioned earlier, confidence can be built quickly, especially when you use all the systems in this book. The thing is, it's rare for you to spend money on something or somebody you don't have any confidence in. Do you? And it's the same for others.

So how do we know confidence is building? One of the best ways of knowing is that they start asking some good buying questions. Not the "how much is it" question. I mean real buying questions. When they start asking, "If I order today, how long will it take" that's them testing us. They want confidence in your answers to know you are the right person to deal with. If they do buy today, will it give them what they want? Does it solve their problem or fulfil their needs? They're asking because they want more confidence in us. They are moving into their buying mode.

Remember, confidence is the first level that people will buy. So we can close a confident customer when they start engaging and asking all the right questions about our business, products, and services. And when they're confident in us and our products and services, we have a good chance of getting a yes, a sale and a client.

A confident mind is fantastic. It's where the magic happens. This is where we get clients. But remember, the 4 levels start again after the sale. They were confident and said yes during the sales process, but now they are clients, meaning we will either maintain this level or take them up to the belief level or, if things go wrong, all the way back to the closed level. So we spend our time after the sale maintaining our relationships with clients and building more and more confidence. To be honest. This is the best level of the human mind. It's where it's best to maintain clients. Someone who has confidence in us and our products and services is also confident they will do more transactions with us.

This is what successful people say, do, and when.

4. Belief Minds

Believers are awesome, and they believe in everything we do. I have my favourite coffee shops, restaurants, clothes, surfboards, cars, and products I know to satisfy me every time, and I tell all my friends that the best are those because I am a believer.

That's the difference between confidence and belief levels. Think of some of the things that you genuinely believe in. I bet you've got a whole heap of them. You've got certain food products, brands, sports teams or disciplines, the things you tell everyone about. We've all got things we believe in, and their competition can't entice our loyalty away from them, can they?

And it takes time to get people to a belief level. It's a great level to get clients to, and what generally happens at the belief level? Those people also give us referrals and tell others they should use our products and services, that ours are the best!

Our conversation with believers is entirely different to every other level. For example, a believer in ReNet didn't ask for a quote on our services. Instead, they would phone up and say I want X, tell me how much, how long, and then do it! They wanted us to deliver it, and they only asked us. We would then use our mud map tactics to manage their time and expectations and provide whatever they asked.

When conversing with someone who believes in our products and services, we talk to them differently. For example, "Hey Tom, we have a new product. It will suit you". Believers reply, "No worries, Scotty, just do it" because they're at the belief level. I had created an environment whereby they trusted that whatever I said was good for their business was good for their business!

Here's the thing, years and years of experience have taught me that with the 4 Levels of the Human Mind, people will go up at only one level at a time but go down all levels at once. They climb from closed to open, open to confident, and then confident to belief. But the bad news is, they always go straight back down to closed from whatever level they were at. Imagine an eight-year client, then something happens, and they leave and never return. Why? Because they totally lost belief, and when they lose belief, they lose trust and don't go back down to confidence or open. No, they go right back down to closed. It happens, but when this happened at ReNet, I knew the system and the journey with the new provider, so we set in motion subtle tactics to win them back, and about 14% of our sales each year were clients returning, proving that using these systems is smart.

So what are the best ways to manage people at the belief level? First, don't convince ourselves we can do anything with these people. If we don't respect them, they will not stay loyal or believers long. So the best way to manage sales and clients is to treat them confidently. Do not over-believe that people will always be at the belief level. If we don't nurture them at the belief level, return the belief and reward them, looking after them by giving belief clients special treatment, then there's only one direction from the belief level, they go right back to closed-minded.

Look after your believers, it's hard to get them there, but they are fantastic for your business. All great businesses have a team of believers they can rely on, and that's perfect Business Judo® too.

In Action

Everything system in this book is about systems to take people on a journey through the 4 levels. The 4 Levels of the Human Mind is the foundation system of what to say, do, and when. The words closed, open, confident, and belief are spread throughout this book. In everyday life, so get used to responding to others at their level. Take a look around you and think about the 4 levels. Ask yourself these;

What levels am I on personally? What levels are my clients at with me and my products? What levels do I notice when I am out buying?

This is what successful people say, do, and when.

SYSTEM 5

The Power of Great Questions

Every year, my sons would ask me, "Is Santa real"?

I would never lie. I'd reply, "Yes, Santa's real". Regardless of our religious beliefs, all you have to do is look around in December every year and see Santa everywhere. Santa exists. What's not real is that Santa goes around the world in a slay delivering presents down a chimney.

Then in 2008, after easter, my eldest son asked, "Is it you that bought the easter eggs"? I said, "Yes". He had just asked the right questions. Then he asked, "You also buy the Christmas presents too"? Again I said "Yes". Finally, he asked the right question, so he got the right answer.

But in business, we depend on questions, but if we ask the wrong questions, we will get the wrong answers in reply. The good news is that I have excellent systems for your questions and some simple rules. And I encourage you to learn these for business and leadership, not just sales. The power of great questions is relevant everywhere in our lives.

In business, It's said that if we find the problems, we can create solutions and sell them. And that's absolutely true. When we solve a problem, life in sales is way easier because people have something they need a solution for. The issue here is that people are told to find problems, which means they often interrogate people to find problems, to the point that they close off the customers.

I see many sales trainers teaching a system of asking lots of questions to find problems. But it's about the right questions. Wrong questions will only get negative responses. Direct questions feel like an interrogation and will lead to negative reactions. But positive questions make a comfortable environment for buyers. So you need a system of great questions asked at the right time to make people comfortable buying in your environment.

So get ready. Make notes here in your workbook. This chapter often redefines everything you have ever known about questions. Things will never be the same again.

The Golden Rule

"Never ask a question that you don't know the answer to!"

Want to get rid of somebody? Then ask a question that shuts them down, closes them off by offending or making them feel stupid! I know it's not anyone's intention as a salesperson to do that, but it happens. Yet, breaking the golden rule is the biggest mistake salespeople make. That is, asking the wrong questions at the wrong time and closing a person off. But it's not the fault of a salesperson. It's the fault of sales training. **Salespeople are trained, not born.** They are taught to ask lots of questions. So it's the right questions at the right time. So allow me to teach you the right way; this is one of the most powerful systems for you, so you know what to say, do, and when.

> *Never ask a question that you don't know the answer to!*

Now let me explain this to you this way. When we're asking a question we don't know the answer to, we leave ourselves exposed to receiving a negative response or, worse, having a lead feel like we are interrogating them. Both lead to negative reactions and more chances of a 'no' answer or objections. So there is a better way to question and not interrogate or get negative responses.

Let me give a real example from ReNet. We would receive enquiries asking, "How much is ReNet"? "How much do you charge to build a website"? Most salespeople would ask questions in reply like, "What's your budget"? And that's so wrong. Why? It's a question I don't know the answer to, do I? Yet I understand why people ask this sort of question in reply, and it almost seems logical to ask what their budget is when someone asks open pricing questions, and salespeople think they need to answer this question, but they don't. It's not important what their budget is. And asking about the budget goes against the golden rule. We will find out the budget soon enough. I will often use the "how much is it" question in this book as it is a perfect example of real-life situations.

So how do we avoid asking questions we don't know the answers to?

You flip it!

You give them the answers. Then ask about the answers.

As an example, "How much is it"? My reply is, "Our products have A, B, & C, come in S, M & L, and can do X, Y, & Z! Most popular is A with M and Z. Which of these are you most interested in"?

See how I gave them the answers first, ABC, SML and XYZ. Yes, they may come back with something else, not the answers I gave, and that's perfect because they can. That's the actual goal here, and I absolutely want them to come back and engage with their questions. What I don't want to do is for them to feel stupid or close them off because of a question I don't know the answer to, like "What's your budget"?

Let me give a better example of how I answered the "how much is it" question at ReNet. Watch how I do this by giving them the answers and then asking a question about the answers I gave. I would typically make a statement like this, "Happy to get you a great price. ReNet specialises in modern website design, advanced CRM, comprehensive XML services, integrated print and e-brochures for marketing, so we have five different specialties for you in real estate". Now I'll ask about the statement and answers I just gave. "Which of these services is important to you, or are you the most interested in getting a price on"?

See what am I doing? I have given them the answers (my products and services), then asked a question about those answers, which will get me a positive response. Generally, leads would start talking about why they needed a new website and their pricing had been forgotten. Why? Because I engaged them and allowed them to ask more questions, I directed their minds to our solutions to their problems rather than how much money they needed to spend. When we solve a problem, sales are a lot easier. Allowing them to ask questions will not make them feel stupid. See how I did that? I asked a question that had answers I knew, as I gave them the answers and then got them to ask about them.

It may appear that I am answering them with a question, but this is not the case, as I am giving them the answers first. I didn't want to answer their question with a question or put them into a corner by asking something stupid like, "How much is your budget"? Their budget does not matter. Only the solution to their problem matters.

So when someone asks something like, "How much is it"? Please don't talk about their budgets. Instead, you need to know their hot spot, the pain and problems they are trying to solve, or their needs. Once we hear their hot spot, pain, or need, then the pricing is straightforward. So give leads your answers first and then let them talk or ask questions about those answers. It takes less work, builds confidence and leads to sales.

So the golden rule is, "Never ask a question that we don't know the answer to." We give them the answers first! And the real magic? That's invoking questions from them instead. This is what successful people do. They get the prospect to ask questions rather than interrogate with their questions, and to do that. They use Sccrates' Successful Method.

This is what successful people say, do, and when.

Socrates Successful Method

It would be great if there were an easy way to get more yes answers and make more money. Wouldn't it?

Then when someone buys from us without us having to do any selling, our life is much easier. True?

And if I showed you a system that does that, you would want to know about it. Wouldn't you?

And those three questions above are an example of Socrates Successful Method. This system was drummed into my head through the 90s, and I teach it because it works.

So what is Socrates Successful Method? I am glad you asked!

> **If you ask a <u>question</u> or a series of <u>questions</u> to which your prospect will readily <u>agree</u>, then ask a concluding <u>question</u> based on those <u>agreements</u>, you will obtain a <u>positive response</u>.**

And that makes sense. Think about it. If we get someone to say yes, yes, yes, and then we ask them a yes question, there is more chance they will say yes, true? Do you remember the old toast example we did as kids? We get someone to say toast 20 times (try it), then ask, "What do you put in a toaster" and the person would say "toast", but we put bread in a toaster. So why did they say toast? Because they were conditioned with toast! And that is how Socrates Successful Method works, and it's not about brainwashing people. It's about leveraging a system that helps people to make a favourable decision to buy from us and not buy from our competition.

Now let's extend this to the golden rule and merge that with Socrates Successful Method like this. First, replace questions with positive statements or a series of statements to which your prospect will readily agree, then make a concluding statement.

> **If you make a <u>statement</u> or a series of <u>statements</u> to which your prospect will readily <u>agree</u>, then make a concluding <u>statement</u> based on those <u>agreements</u>, you will obtain a <u>positive response</u>.**

Let's reverse this. Imagine asking questions that give a 'no", or we make statements that give us a negative response. What's going to happen? We would probably get a 'no' answer. And that's not what we want. We want yes answers, true?

Let me give a funny coffee example of sometimes when it was my turn to shout coffee. I'd walk up to the others and say, "You don't want a coffee, do you"? What do you think the answer was? Yep, a much bigger chance of a 'no'. But if I'd say, "I would love another coffee. Would you like me to get you one too"? There is more chance they'll say, 'yes'.

It's the same thing with selling. We've got to ask the right questions at the right times to create an environment where people want to buy. And Socrates Successful Method is the system used to get more yes answers. You need as many positive responses as possible. That's how you have constructive and intentional conversations that help people buy in your environment, not with your competition.

The 3 Reasons to Ask

We now know from Socrates Successful Method that we will obtain a positive response when we ask a series of positive questions. And we also know we will get negative responses when we ask negative

This is what successful people say, do, and when.

questions. So we replace questions with statements as nobody wants to ask negative questions or get negative responses, do they?

At about now, most people ask me, "But how do I find out what they want"? "I have been taught to ask lots of questions to find their problems", and they're right. But by now, you understand why question time is very fragile or sensitive in your buying environment.

The thing is that there are only 3 reasons why we ask questions. Generally, good questions come back to understanding what the 4 Levels of the Human Mind are or even what zone they're in, the warm or hot zone (and more on the zones later).

So what are the ONLY 3 reasons why we ask questions?

1. **To obtain a positive response.**

2. **To direct a prospect's mind.**

3. **To obtain information.**

1. **To obtain a positive response.** And we do want positive responses, don't we? So we have to ask positive questions to get a positive response. So using short, sharp, positive questions works great in obtaining a positive response. And quick is good.

2. **To direct the lead's mind.** Sometimes we have to ask questions to lead them one way or the other. We must also combine this with the Golden Rule and Socrates Successful Method. We are making those positive statements about our products and following up with questions directing them to our products and services.

3. **To obtain information.** We need to ask questions to get information. Often these are information questions at the end of the sale system and when people have gained enough confidence to buy, like confirming colours and sizes. You can ask those while you are locking in a deal.

Here's something that happened to me recently, I wanted to engage a photographer. I wanted them to "do and charge" because I had seen their work. He insisted on a Zoom call. I was OK with that and was happy they wanted to understand my needs first. During that call, they asked many unnecessary questions, and even so, I entertained and answered them. After all, he is the expert, and I wanted to buy. Then they said they had a questionnaire I needed to fill out. Now they were starting to lose me. They already mentioned that pricing was $700 for the shoot and said OK, but they persisted with the questionnaire. This breaks nearly all the question rules. But, once again, I entertained it, filled it out straight away and sent it back within minutes, and although succinctly, I still answered them. But why? I was saying yes, and it was an easy sale, so why did they make it so hard for me to buy?

If they needed to know more, they could have closed the sale, and then asked me to fill out his questionnaire, or even done it for me, then booked me in (using the 7-time tactics of successful people). But no, I still have not paid or done a photo shoot yet. So their reasons are honourable, they wanted information, but their system needs to be fixed. Imagine how many sales they lose by using this interrogation system. He could have asked me for payment, sealed the deal, and then sent me his questionnaire, but instead, his questions became a roadblock and, ultimately, a lost sale. Oh, they did eventually respond to me with this.

I've been racking my brain about exactly what to shoot for you, and I just can't nail down a range of images for you.

I was still wanting to buy it, so I said…

Up to you, but we can make it work. I am not that fussy. A bunch of beach and studio, it will be easy.

I still had no response at the time of writing, yet I was saying yes. I can only hope it was because their business was booming, and they preferred more qualified clients.

My point is this. When responding to people, we must consider the questions we use. What are those questions? Are they roadblocks? Are they even necessary? Could they lead to negative responses in our buying environment? So only ask questions to get positive responses, direct the lead's mind, or obtain (required) information. Yet people are

This is what successful people say, do, and when.

often taught to ask questions and lots of them in sales. So make a note of the questions you ask and what the reactions are. Great questions take practice and time to perfect, but it's worth it when people say yes to you quicker, and you're achieving and making more money.

Keeping it Going

Questions are great for conversation continuation. As in, we get them to ask us to keep talking to them; would you like me to explain more?

When in conversation (written or verbal), and someone asks for more information, we can ask a continuing question such as, "Is that OK"? For example, "I will get you a sample. Is that OK"? "I will do some research and get back to you next week. Is next week OK"?

As an example, answer to "How much is it"? Try "Let me get some examples for pricing. I will be back in a minute. Is that OK"?

Generally, with these positive continuation questions, and because they are open questions, and we offer to do something for them, the answer will almost always be positive. Someone will rarely say "don't" or "no". So it's a great use of positive questions and the flow of our presentations and conversations.

This is also perfect Business Judo®, as they ask us to do more for them. We have flipped the narrative; they are becoming engaged and involved in our buying environment.

Be Rhetorical

In other words, ask questions that we don't need the answer to or that we assume their answer will be a yes or a positive response. This is one of the best systems to use for questions.

When they talk or answer back, we have asked a question in the right way. And we want their positive response, don't we?

Did you see how I did that?

You answered yes, didn't you?

This is what successful people say, do, and when.

Did you see how I did that again?

Now you have said yes three times in 10 seconds, and that's the best use of questions ever! Yet they were all rhetorical questions. So I don't need your answer, but I probably still obtained your positive response.

"But Scotty, what if someone answers and is negative or asks about something different"? OK, good question, and that can happen. And it's good news when it does because they have flipped our conversation and are now talking about what they really want, and that's what we want to know, true?

Let me give a negative answer to a car salesperson (**SP**) example.

SP: "The red metallic colour of this car looks great, doesn't it"?

Me: "I don't like red. I like blue"!

That's not a negative answer. On the contrary, it's perfect, and here is why!

SP: "Good news, we have two different blue options for you. Can I show you"?

Let me give you a positive Ford Salesman example.

SP: "The red metallic colour of this car looks great, doesn't it"?

Me: "It looks great. But do you have other colours"?

It's the same answer, isn't it?

SP: "I am glad you mentioned it. We have many different colour options for you. Can I show you"?

Now, this seems simple, but it does take time to perfect. Here is a simple list of rhetorical questions that achieve this.

Right?

True?

Isn't it?

Correct?

Isn't it?

Doesn't it?

Isn't that right?

Isn't that good?

Isn't that true?

Now list all the ones you prefer to use, then assimilate them into your conversations.

If they do answer, let them talk, as that's when you find out more information.

Questioning a Question

I bet car dealers get asked, "How much is a new car"?

I bet builders get asked, "How much is a new house"?

I bet resorts get asked, "How much is accommodation"?

When someone asks, "How much"? And then we ask, "How much is your budget"? That's an excellent example of a lousy question answering a question. **Questioning their questions does not answer their question.** Questioning their questions gets us nowhere and creates a negative, damaging or hostile environment.

Why? People don't know how much they want to spend; even if they do, they don't want to say. Also, the how much is it question really is them saying, "I don't know or understand yet. Can you explain it to me". Successful salespeople understand that the moment someone asks a question, that's the chance for them to open a lead's mind and build their confidence in them and their products. And when someone asks a successful salesperson, "How much"? They understand that a lead is asking, "Can you tell me more about what I get for my money"?

We welcome their questions as that's how they go through their buying process, and when they ask questions, they are in their buying mode. So be very careful and avoid answering their question with a

This is what successful people say, do, and when.

question and pushing them out of their buying mood and ultimately, your buying environment.

So what's the best way to NOT answer a question with a question? Instead, we answer questions with statements. Answer questions with positive sentences using Socrates Successful Method and FAB (more on FAB soon), discussing features and the advantages and benefits.

For example, this would happen all the time at ReNet. Real estate agents would ask, "How much is a new website"? We can't answer that, can we? A simple agent website could be $1,000 or $20,000. We didn't ask them how much money they had or their budget, so we would go into a presentation with other websites we had built, allowing them to talk about their hot spot, pain, or need. Once we know these, we then had better ways of answering their questions through conversations about what we do.

So, what can you do? First, write down questions that you get all the time, then work out how to answer those questions and direct them the way you want, and lead them through a positive conversation that opens their mind about your products and services that you do have and avoid answering a question with a question.

If you feel compelled to ask a question, then here is a question you may ask, and it honours all the other systems you have seen so far.

"Can you tell me more (about their question)… "?

This is a question, and you can use this as a question when they ask stupid questions. The important thing is that we don't ask them stupid questions back.

For example:

Q: "How much is a new website"?

A: "Can you tell me more about the websites you're interested in"?

Q: "How much is a new house"?

A: "Tell me more about the house you like to build"?

This is what successful people say, do, and when.

Q: "How much is accommodation"?

A: "Tell me more about the accommodation you want to book"?

Can you see how that works? I have only questioned what I already know and what they are asking about. And this involves them. And it gets us more information. So, see how this is an excellent use of the question, "Can you tell me more about…"?

Negotiation is Buying

"I hate it when people ask for a discount," someone said to me once, and then they said, "My price is my price". But that showed me they don't understand the system or the psychology of a buyer.

When someone starts to buy, especially in larger transactions, they will often begin to test us as part of their negotiation, which is good news. These tests can be simple as asking, "What's your best price"? Or "Can I have it today"? Or "How long does it take to get started"? Or "Will it take long"? These are all buying and negotiation questions from them. The buyer is looking for reasons to say yes or no. So don't be offended when someone wants to negotiate. Expect it.

No matter how you look at it, negotiation is always someone potentially saying yes and buying from you!

Some salespeople get offended when a buyer tries to negotiate or makes an offer to buy at a discount rate. Remember, they are going on the journey of the 4 Levels of the Human Mind. People won't say they are yet to understand the value (more about this later). When they start negotiating, they are looking to close and either say yes or no. So you are close to the closing stage of the cycle, so you better ensure they have enough information as you negotiate a close so you don't lose them.

When I sold insurance, there was no negotiation, and the price was the price. But when I sold ReNet to real estate agents, what did they do for a living? Negotiate deals! So it was expected that deals would be done. And if they ever mentioned that something was expensive, I say with humour, "How else am I going to afford a luxury car like real

This is what successful people say, do, and when.

estate agents, hahaha", and then we'd get back to finalise a deal. So don't be scared of the price negotiation questions.

Negotiation doesn't have to be on price! We all want a bargain, and people want to know if this is the best possible deal. So think of negotiation as them saying, "I want to buy". But it's just a couple of terms that I'm looking for. So from your side, avoid negotiating on price, negotiate on delivery times, extras and value add, deliverables, yep, there are lots of things other than price.

So expect a negotiation, appreciate it, and understand it's a yes! Everything we have done to achieve a sale has gotten us to this closing point, the yes and the negotiation. Remember, very few people will say, "I don't understand the value yet. Can you give me your presentation again". So welcome negotiation because that means we're on the home straight and have done everything right, although we may still need to give more value for their money.

But a word of warning, if someone starts negotiating at the introduction stage, and you haven't done your presentation yet, and they ask, "Can I get a discount"? This is because they are still saying, "I want more information", and not "Can I buy"? So be careful NOT to start negotiating before explaining all your value propositions.

Are You Sure?

"I'd like to think about it". I've seen salespeople respond with, "Are you sure"? This is what they hear when asked that: "Are you stupid"?

I have done thousands of hours of field training with salespeople, and it was amazing how many people asked, "Are you sure"? It's a dead-set conversation stopper. It's a terrible habit! Go back to the golden rule, or the 3 reasons we ask questions, or answer a question with a question. "Are you sure" does not work. Although we get a yes answer, in this case, it's a positive "yes" to their "no", and the show is over.

See what just happened with the 4 Levels of the Human Mind? The salesperson just took them to closed-minded because they were now

This is what successful people say, do, and when.

questioning their intelligence and decision-making. "Are you sure" is a useless question that does nothing to benefit anyone.

When buyers say "I'd like to think about it", it's buyers saying, "Can I have more information". Or "I'd like to think about it", which may even mean in the next 5 minutes too, so right now is the best opportunity to help them think about it. I will show more about responding to the "I'll think about it" question later in the book when we go through the close in the business and sales cycle.

You Get Back to Me

Imagine a fisherman who has a fish on his line. He catches it and then lets it go because he hopes to catch it again tomorrow. If he does, great, but what are the chances of a fisherman catching that fish twice?

There's an old saying. If we love something, set it free. If they come back, they are ours. If they don't, they never were.

So in sales, when we let someone go, and they do come back, they definitely want to buy, so there is truth to that. And making clients come back is an excellent qualifier of interest. But this is not really how things work in sales. Your income depends on how easy it is for people to buy, not how hard it is.

When I hear people say something like "You get back to me" or "Phone me when you are ready" as an answer to "I want to think about it" or "Maybe next week", it makes me cringe. It's important not to let leads go from our zones. They are in our hot or warm zone; we need to retain them there, not let them go (more on zones soon). It's so much easier to sell to someone right in front of us now than to market trying to find more opportunities.

So what do we do when someone needs more time? Some people do want to think about it. Our objective must be to keep buyers in our warm zone for as long as possible and not let them go or push them away as clients. It's up to us to keep the process and conversation going if we want their business. That's what professional salespeople do.

This is what successful people say, do, and when.

SELL MORE MAKE MORE - The Best Sales Systems Ever!

The worst thing we can do is "Let them get back to us". We get back to them unless we don't care about their business. Being a successful salesperson means we don't let them go or leave our zones and maintain control of our buying environment, our warm zone! Instead, we can give them follow-up calls, go into our customer pipeline, and use the Rule of 100™ as a perfect follow-up system.

The point is, **do not let them go**. Keep them feeling like they are in control, yet we try and set the pace of what's next. It could be as simple as "looking forward to seeing you next week" in small transactions. It would be "I'll give you a call next week" in bigger transactions. See how that's maintaining control of our buying environment. See how easy it is to replace "You get back to me"?

I have met some salespeople that have a three-strike rule. They say "I'm not going to ring any more than three times, if they want it they can contact me"! That's one way of qualifying people. If they contact us back, that sure means they do want it. So there's some truth to that! I totally get it. And yes, there is a point where it's just not worth following up on anymore. But that's not the point! If someone you spoke to last year wants to buy from you this year, you would like that, wouldn't you? So the people you are talking to today may well become your clients next year. The point is that if these people are still in our warm zone, then they are still in our opportunity third in the Business of Thirds®. They are worth holding on to. So please keep them in the palm of your hands. If they want a product or a service like yours, then why not yours? Why let them go? A sale next week is just as good as a sale today. So nurture them, keep them warm, and keep them where you want them to be, in your buying environment, not with your competition. Remember the worst outcome in sales: someone buys your products and services but gives their money to someone else. So if they buy from you next week or next year, that's OK. Just try not to let them go out of your buying environment.

This is what successful people say, do, and when.

Any Questions?

This question, "Any questions," seems like a great question. But it's a bad habit, let me explain why. People often say or write this in emails, "Let me know if you have any questions," as their email sign-off or close. Now it does seem like a great question to finish with, and I understand why it's used. We do want to help someone with questions, don't we? So this seems so supportive. But in selling, it's not! It doesn't do anything positive to close a conversation. It's as bad as "You get back to me". So where is the what's next? And it passes control back to the client because it says, "Let me know". The point here is that this gives complete control back to the client! So what's the best way to do this?

The best answer is to mud map it and have reasons to contact them back. We create a reason to keep them in our warm zone. Think about it, if a lead has any questions, they generally ask. But when we pass control back to them or push them out of our warm zone, it's much harder for us to get them back.

The answer is to say things that keep the momentum going, such as "Looking forward to delivering ABC", "We'll talk next week", or "I'll give you a quick follow-up next week, and I'll let you know how I've gone", or "I'm going to do a bit more research and give you a call back". With a quick finish with "Talk soon". See how these keep leads open-minded and in our warm zone? Their response tells us if they are still interested or if they're really just trying to say "no" nicely, and if that's the case, we can let them go. Selling is about strike rates, and keeping the momentum going with all leads is essential to a successful sales system. I will discuss this further when I show the follow-up systems later.

The point is, when we let them leave our environment, they may go into someone else's, and if they're thinking about buying our products and services, we want them to buy from us.

We're the salesperson, the expert, and we get back to them!

This is what successful people say, do, and when.

The Power in You

The fact is that questions make and break sales, and this one system alone is responsible for more failed sales than successful outcomes. Why? Because this is the most fragile time in our conversations. I could spend six months perfecting questions for an organisation, and more work would still need to be done.

You have the power to perfect your questions. To improve my sales conversations, I used a digital recorder and recorded my conversations. Maybe you could record your conversations as I did, or write your questions down and work on perfecting them. That power of great questions relies on you.

People who perfect their questions have the power to achieve more sales and make so much more money with the same, and often less work.

The power of questions is how you have them to ask more questions than you. In other words, don't ask lots of questions. Seek the answers!

SYSTEM 6

So What?

People want what it does, not what it is!

Meaning people buy what it does, not what it is!

In other words, they can see what it is, but why should they buy your products from you? So answering the "so what" question is one of the most important things to do in sales.

I have a product, "so what"?

I have a service, "so what"?

When you start to look at your products and services with a "so what" mindset, it's a game changer. What is it? That's easy. Most people can see what things are, but "so what"? We must answer that in everything we do. So what means you must ask yourself questions like this; What will it do for them? And what does that mean to them?

The good news is that there is an excellent system for answering the 'so what' question. It's called Features - Advantages - Benefits (**FAB**).

Let's dive in.

FAB

FAB is a popular system because it makes it easy to answer your so what questions about what you do and why so people understand.

FAB is so easy to remember. It allows customers to understand the advantages of your products and services, and they know their benefits.

FAB is a sales system that works and will always work in sales as leads want to know more about what they are buying and why it will solve their problems or fulfil their needs.

FAB addresses the 'so what' question people think while buying something. When we are presenting, we believe people are listening, but they want to know what it will do for them and talking about benefits does that for them.

Now I just did four FABs for you. Yep, the four opening paragraphs above are examples. Each paragraph above has a feature, advantage and benefit of FAB.

I remember going into a computer store in 2006 to buy a PDA. Before smartphones, a PDA was a Personal Digital Assistant with an electronic diary and contact list. About 15-20 PDAs with different prices and brands were displayed on the wall. Each one had its cardboard A4 description card beside it, all the features in bullet point format, a standard in all electronic stores. I asked the salesman, "Can you tell me more about the PDAs"? He then read out the cardboard bullet points to me. I started thinking, and I didn't say I couldn't read! I could read the signs, but so what? This salesperson didn't have a system, and he wasn't taught a way of explaining any 'so what' or what were the differences and why they'd be good for me. And FAB does that.

Features: What is it?

Advantages: What does the feature do?

Benefits: What does the feature mean to them personally?

This is what successful people say, do, and when.

Forget the Features!

OK, don't actually forget features, but features anyone can see. People can see it's a red or black car and has leather or cloth trim. They can read the sign in the electronic shop. They can see what colour pens are for sale. And mostly, they can see features in your products and services too. But when someone asks us a question about a product, what they really want to know is, "So what"? What is the advantage of it and then the benefit to them? So anytime you talk about features, you need to talk about the advantages and benefits of that feature too, or "so what"? The advantages and benefits are what make people buy. They buy the advantage of the feature and the benefit for themselves.

Using the Business of Thirds® system (one of the 5 Systems of Successful People), those leads in the middle third can go either way depending on how we have a constructive conversation and our presentation. Well, this is where FAB comes into its own. FAB mentions the features, but, importantly, it romances the advantage of the feature itself and then the benefit to them of that feature.

Yes, we should be feature-rich. That's true! But "so what". And that's when the advantages and benefits come in when competing for someone's business. And what's the difference between advantages and benefits? They're the same thing, aren't they? No, they're not. Let's sell a pen as we go through FAB. Not all pens are the same; if you can FAB a pen, you can FAB anything!

Using Advantages

What's an advantage? That's the advantage of the feature itself.

For example, here's a blue felt tip pen. So what? Or. This blue felt tip pen has the advantage that it's an accepted colour, formal and legal, and your clients can use it too, so everyone's writing is clear with the felt tip. You can see here that I used the word "advantage", so you can literally say it like that if you want as long as you romance the advantage of the feature itself (blue felt tip). I could have shortened it to this. This blue pen is the perfect formal colour for signing all your documents (the advantage of the feature). I still delivered the advantage of being a formal colour. It's just done quicker. See how easy the advantages are?

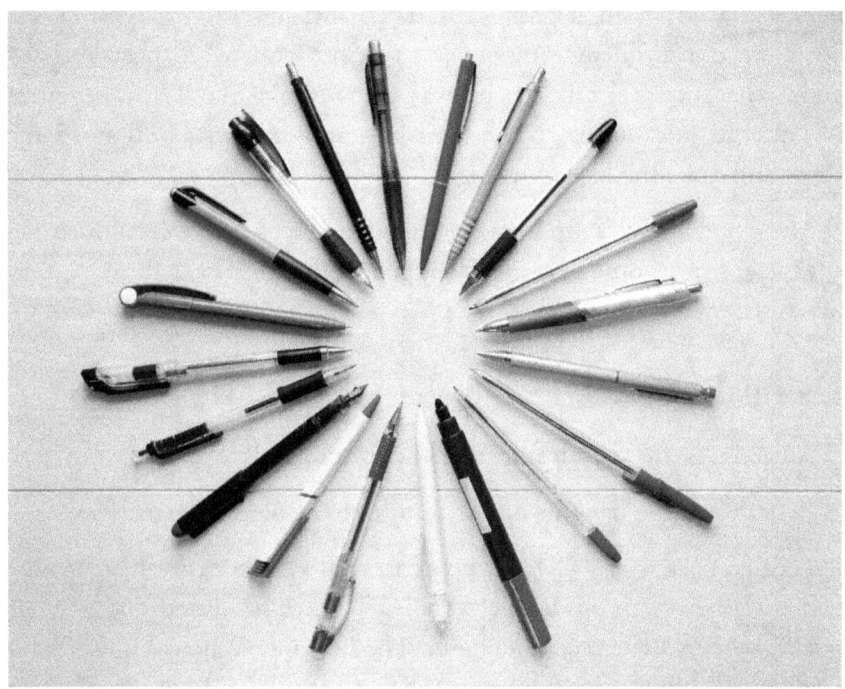

As another example, here's a blue felt tip pen. So what? Or. This blue pen is light and has a lid with a pocket holder so that the pen tip will stay protected and in your pocket when you are out and about (the advantage of the feature).

See how the advantage is the advantages of features, products, or services themselves. This is how we discuss what it is and what it does. Finally, we answer, "So what"? In other words, it's not just a blue pen. It is much more. There's an advantage to being blue.

Another example is the pen type; some have a lid, and others are retractable. What's an advantage of a lid or retractable pen? So what? The lid protects the ballpoint or tip. The retractable slides back in, so the tips are protected by the pen, and you can't lose the lid. Now pick another pen from the above photo. How many features can you come up with regarding the colour, size, lids, tips, etc? Now think about the features and what it really does (its advantage).

Every single product or service has an advantage. It's not just a blue pen, it's not just a lid, it's not just clear plastic, and it's not just a felt tip. So if we don't romance the advantages, how can we expect leads to know what they are? Like when I was trying to buy the PDA. They want to know its advantages so they can buy, and in return, you avoid the show-and-hope method in selling.

The good news is that having this constructive conversation using advantages saves time because when people think, "That's for me", they buy from you.

Using Benefits

Advantages are the advantage of the feature itself.

Benefits are the benefits of the feature to the person themselves.

Let's go back to the blue felt tip pen. What's the benefit of being blue and with a lid? An advantage was that it stays protected and in your pocket when you are out and about. The benefits? When you use it, it's readily available in your pocket, you haven't lost it, and because the pen is protected, it still works when you need it. See the difference. I am now talking about the buyer and their benefit for buying it. I even use and repeat the all important **you** word.

Let's bring FAB together with a sentence using all three.

"This blue felt tip pen has the **advantage** of being formal colour and the **benefit** that you are ready for any documents that need signing".

"This blue pen has a lid for your pocket, so you don't lose it, and it is protected when dropped, meaning it will always be in mint condition when you need it".

These are simple examples of selling a pen. Now think about the features of your product and their advantages and then the benefits to your clients. Next, create a list and then turn your FAB list into a series of descriptive sentences. Now practice how to say them and be ready for when you need them.

Note: You can do FAB or FBA, just as long as you address the "so what" question. You romance the "how can you benefit from buying this"? And with practice, it will roll off the tongue, and nobody will know you are using the FAB system. It will seem natural. Most people will say things like, "You really know your stuff. Thank you"!

For example, take a look at how they sell shampoo using FAB. Can you see how many times they used it?

WIIFM (What's in it for me?)

Every person we talk to has WIIFM written across the top of their head. At least, that's what I want you to imagine, and they want to know; What's In It For Me?

So what? Why should I listen?

So what? What are the advantages and benefits?

So what? What's in it for me?

Remember these questions in every sales conversation. There is no exception to WIIFM. And need to constantly address "what's in it for them" in our products and sales!

This is what successful people say, do, and when.

For example:

What time is this going to save me?

What problem is this solving for me?

What's the feeling this is going to give me?

Sales it's all about them. Use WIIFM to your advantage to help you explain products to them in a way they understand. The more you think like them and ensure you are answering WIIFM, and the more you answer their so what questions, the more you will improve your strike rate in sales. Number 1 on System 1357® is people first. People over everything. It's not what it is. It's what's in it for them!

No FAB in the Competition

Who cares about the competition anyway? You don't get paid for their sales, do you? You only get paid from yours!

The good news is that it's your lucky day if a lead is talking to you about your competition because that means your competitor didn't get the sale, and now you can! This is because they have come into your warm zone, and your competitor lost them from theirs.

But how do we get around talking about the competition when a lead mentions them?

What happens is that salespeople tend to get drawn into their conversation about the competition, and I've seen this happen (a lot). Of course, you can't ignore the competition when a lead brings them up, but we should never talk about the competition in return, either good or bad. Why? You are not selling their products. You can only sell yours! So do not engage in that conversation. This seems so obvious, but salespeople do it all the time.

Let me give an example, a car salesperson. I walk into the Ford dealer and start saying something about a Toyota I've been looking at. When the Ford dealer starts talking to me about Toyota, what are they doing? They're talking about a Toyota. What are they selling, Ford? What's the benefit of a Ford salesman talking about Toyota? Nothing! So all that matters is that he talks about Ford. That's it! It does not matter if I do or don't like Toyota or if I am positive or negative about Toyota. The Ford salesman needs to concentrate on me. I am in their zone right now. I didn't buy a Toyota, did I? But there is an opportunity to buy a Ford if done right.

As a salesperson, we talk only about what we can and do sell.

There is one possible exception to this rule, and that's when they are negative. You may quickly reinforce a negative and concrete it back to them. So if someone came to me as a Ford salesman and said they were looking at a Toyota but didn't like its shape, I may say something like, "I hear that many people don't like the shape either". Then segway back to my Fords. And that's not talking about Toyota. It's reinforcing the negative to them, and then I would redirect them back to what people like about Ford. See how that can work. But be very careful. It's a fine line. So it's still best to simply use the comment as a segway to jump straight into what other people like about Fords and ignore the comment.

I am saying that you try **not** to talk about your competition at all, and even if I, as a lead, keep talking about Toyota, the Ford salesman should just let me finish, get it all off my chest, and then segway what I am talking about back into Ford.

If they had wanted to buy the competition's product, they would have bought it already, but they didn't! So now it's your turn. Are you the better salesperson?

Now What?

So now you know, now you have to do, that's what! First, write down a list of all the features you have in your products and services, then write beside those what the advantage of the feature is, and then write down the benefits to the buyer. Next, look at everything you get asked about them and devise constructive and structured sentences to talk about them. Next, you need to answer buyers 'so what' questions, what's good about it, and what does it do for me?

Use the below form in your workbook to create your FAB sentences.

Feature	Advantage	Benefit
Itself...	Of the feature	To the person
What is it?	What does it do?	What does it mean to them?

SYSTEM 7

Zones

This is an unreal system, your cold, warm, and hot zones?

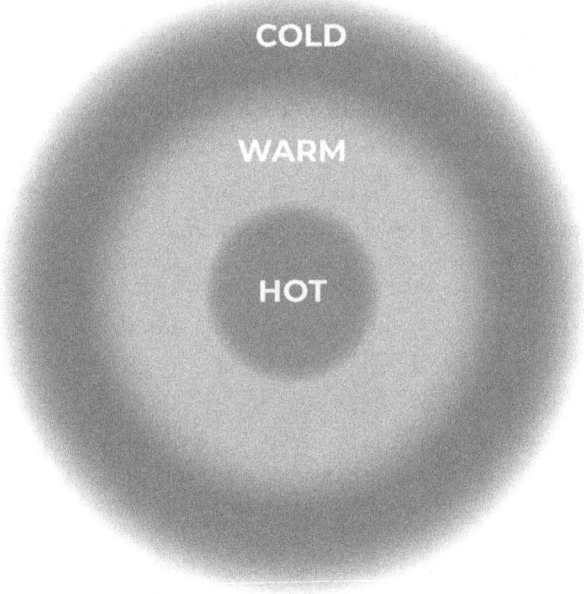

You have already seen me talk about these zones earlier in the book. Now let me give the back story of where the cold, warm, and hot zones came from. I was in the fire brigade as a first responder for almost eight years. And when we arrived at a fire, we established three zones. First, where the fire is, that's the hot zone. Then immediately around the hot zone is the warm zone, where the fire truck is parked, the police, the ambulance and anyone else involved in the fire. So the warm zone is where a lot of the action actually happens. Then, outside of that is the

This is what successful people say, do, and when.

cold zone, where all the general public and those not involved directly in the fire are.

And we have precisely identical zones in sales and business. So, for example, the cold zone is where we do marketing, the warm zone is where we do the selling, and the hot zone is when the sale becomes a client,

Or another way of saying it is that we do marketing for people in the cold zone to bring them into our warm zone, and then in the warm zone, we do all our presentations and closing trying to get them into our hot zone, which is a customer.

Let's look at a life cycle example of our friendly Ford dealer. First, they do their marketing and launch a specials campaign to attract people from the cold zone. Then we decide we want to consider a Ford, and that's when we enter their warm zone, the dealership. Next, we become clients and enter their hot zone if they do everything right. So people physically come from the cold, through the warm and into the hot zone.

Now let's take it to a new level, zones within zones. Yep, we have micro-zones, too, like at the Ford dealership. There are cold, warm, and hot zones within the dealership too. We are in the cold zone when we walk around the yard. Why? Because we are wandering around on our own. So, where's the warm zone? That's when we are conversing with the salesperson, regardless of where that is. It's when they're selling to us, hopefully listening to what we want, not interrogating us with questions, and listening to our conditions, actions and needs. We are not in the hot zone yet! So what's the hot zone in the dealership? I am glad you asked!

People make buying decisions in the hot zone; it is tough to close someone in the warm zone and literally impossible to close in the cold zone. And in car dealerships, there are multiple hot zones. Let me give two examples.

Firstly, when we test drive a car, we're in the salesperson's hot zone. If we liked the car, we'd probably be excited and be in the buying mode right then, wouldn't we? So sitting or test driving a car is one of the

This is what successful people say, do, and when.

places people decide to buy a car. That's why a car salesperson always wants to tag along.

The most obvious hot zone is when we are sitting at the salesperson's desk. That's why they get us to come inside, sit down, start talking, look at figures, order times, and all sorts of things because it's their hot zone. It's a decision-making zone. So they will offer drinks and incentives to get us into their hot zone because they know how the system works.

When we sit at the salesperson's desk, we know it's decision time. And so do they. So in reverse, this is also the best time to negotiate a better deal because you are in their hot zone. Want a better deal? Business Judo® them and use their zone to your advantage.

Let me give another example. I have done a lot of cold calling, and I'd pull up at someone's house, and I had to think about the zones available to me. I needed to get the prospect to where they make their decisions, which was never at the front door. I had to work out ways to have them open the front door and let me in so I could get to their hot zone inside the house. And then inside the house, that was at the kitchen table, the back deck, and sometimes even a work shed. I needed to quickly work out where they sat as a family and do all their normal talking. Their hot zone is the only place an effective presentation can happen. Why? Because that's where sales happen. I learnt fast that they never purchase in the cold zone, like at the front door. Sometimes a work truck was parked out the front, so I'd use that. Why? It's theirs, and it's where they work all day. So I would do a presentation on their equipment as that's where they make business decisions, and it's their hot zone.

Now think about a retail shop. A retail shop has zones too. Outside the shop is cold, the warm zones are while walking around in the shop looking, and the hot zones are the fitting rooms and cash registers.

Where are your cold, warm, and hot zones in your business? Where are they physically, and how do you treat people in each zone? Successful people treat people differently depending on which one their prospects are in, as zones help them know what to say, do, and when.

This is what successful people say, do, and when.

Cold Zone

Some say they hate coffee catch-ups with people. Often they feel people are stealing their time. People want to have a coffee with them but don't do business with them. That's because they don't understand the prospecting system, nor what to do or how to do it with people in a cold zone environment. This is when it's good to have your knowledge of the 4 Levels of the Human Mind. Closed, open, confident, and belief. I catch up with people all the time and have coffee, sometimes, it's virtually too, and it's amazing how many have become clients two years later. This is because I created a need and understood my zones.

We must treat people in the cold zone with an open mind having open conversations to keep their minds open. Assume everybody in the cold zone wants to come into the warm zone at some point. All the systems in this book are so we can transition leads through the zones. And the cold zone is **not** where we sell or close. So prospecting, with open, suggestive conversations, attracts them into our environment, allowing them to physically move into our warm zone in the sales system or our physical warm zone at our location. So sales or buying conversations happen in your warm zone. So even a catchup coffee in a cafe is in your warm zone because it's a conversation.

The cold zone is called the cold zone for a reason. We have to warm people up. And how do we warm people up? That is by being friendly and open, and warm. Consider where they are and whether it's the right time in our buying environment. Do we need to schedule a better time, come back, or do something else? If I couldn't get to someone's warm or hot zone when cold calling, I left nicely and made a quick and sharp plan to return later when I had a second chance at getting out of the cold zone.

Take a networking event as an example. Conversations may seem to be in a warm zone at that event, but it's physically in everyone's cold zone. So it's best to reschedule to catch up somewhere in someone's warm zone or a warm neutral zone. Not in that cold zone.

This is what successful people say, do, and when.

Sales is the skill of constantly transitioning people through the zones. We want to keep them from going and becoming a client of the competition, don't we? So if it's impossible to meet physically in person, try to get on a video call with them, a virtual coffee, or whatever it takes to get them out of the cold zone.

The good news is that some people transition fast from cold to hot. Because somehow they already know, like, and trust you, and they come along to buy. And that does happen, and enjoy those wins when you get them. But I'm talking about the sales process here. So when they are cold or in the cold zone, having warm conversations helps buyers to know, like, and trust you.

Warm Zone

So much action happens here. Of course, people from here can go back to the cold or enter your hot zone. But you've done all your marketing and prospecting, so now you have someone to talk to. This is when your constructive and intentional conversation or sales presentation happens.

Hopefully, in our conversations, it's them asking many questions. Think back to the 4 Levels of the Human Mind. We lead people on a journey by letting them ask us questions as they transition from open to confident. All that happens in your warm zones. This is where they need more information, as they've transitioned from the cold into your warm zone to get more reasons to buy or not.

We appreciate and respect their time in the warm zone, and we must be more business-like and confidently talk about the products. Treat people in the warm zone like they want to become clients, as if they're already customers and involve them when they do.

Remember the electronic store and the PDAs I spoke about earlier in FAB? I was in the warm zone as he read out the signs to me, but he lost me, and I went cold in his warm zone. I needed him to give me the advantages and benefits of the PDAs. I needed him to go into a conversation and presentation. I was in his warm zone asking to buy

This is what successful people say, do, and when.

products, yet he gave me nothing of value and nothing to answer the "so what" questions, and that's what I bought from him, nothing! I walked out. They had done their marketing and got me out of the cold, yet pushed me back into the cold. Maybe if he'd had training, things would be different. And perhaps if he'd used FAB, he would probably make more sales.

The trick in the warm zone is to know what to say, do, and when so you transition people through the warm zone to get them to your hot zone.

Hot Zone

Have you ever heard of the man chair? That's a chair out the front of a ladies' retail shop. Why do they have it? Because some shop owners know that if they keep the husband happy, the wife can stay in their shop longer. Secondly, they want to keep the men comfortable and out of their hot buying environment so they don't negatively interfere with the sales happening inside the warm and hot zones inside the shop. What a clever tactic that still works today. See above, my mother-in-law had one of these chairs in the 90s at her retail shop, and it worked a treat. OK, the chair can be for anyone, not just men. But we called it the

This is what successful people say, do, and when.

man chair for this reason. And this is a perfect example of all three zones being used systemically to keep everyone happy.

So how do we treat people in the hot zone regarding sales? Think back to the car dealership. This is where prices are negotiated, payments are made, and transactions are completed. And if you are not ready for it or overshoot the zone, it can push people back a zone or two. The hot zone is the only place these actions happen. It's not possible to negotiate pricing in the cold zone. It's not possible to have a successful transaction in the cold zone. It's not possible to deliver products or services in the cold zone. In other words, your hot zone is where your pricing, transactions, and delivery happens.

What about once they say yes and they are now a client? They have decided they like what we do and what we have to offer. Now is when we start showing our appreciation. We stop selling because we want people to stay clients and stay in our hot zone for as long as possible, don't we? That means we need systems to keep clients happy and enjoying who we are as they stay in our environment. We want them to continue buying when they want or need it next. We've done everything we needed to get them into our hot zone, so now it's a matter of protecting them. Like treating them as the valued people they are.

What about the physical hot zone? Remember the car dealer? Their hot zones are test driving or the salesperson's desk. When I was selling and calling on businesses, I did the same, and I always went to a prospect's desk within their business premises. That's their hot zone. It's where they do their business! Remember, at people's homes, it was the dinner table or where they usually sat. I needed to get to where the decision-making process was.

I trained real estate agents on how to achieve more listings. And their hot zones are where they have had other successful transactions. And whenever someone wanted to sell their house, I taught the real estate agent to always go to the homeowner's house because that is the homeowner's hot zone. It's not at the real estate agent's office.

This is what successful people say, do, and when.

The hot zone is the physical or the decision-making zone. Where people decide, "Why should I buy this and from you"? They are hot when they're in their decision-making mindset, asking buying questions and negotiating. The hot zone is where successful transactions are done.

Think about the cold, warm, and hot zones in your business, write them down, and make take advantage of them. Think about your zones within zones too, and how you can take advantage of them.

The Pull Effect

So many people are trying to push us to become their clients: spam, direct messages, push, push, push. There are better ways to think about sales than pitch-slapping. The pull effect means we don't push and work on systems that pull or bring people into our environment instead.

Knowing your zones gives you an advantage because you can use a Pull Effect in your sales systems. In other words, when you push people, you generally push them out. And you pull them in by attracting them and making them comfortable to enter your environment.

In our marketing, we may throw out some offers, a do-it-now, specials, or some last-minute deals. These all have a pull effect on people to bring them out from the cold. So the business and sales cycle I go through later in the book is to attract people, and it's a cycle and an inward vortex. In fact, all the systems in this book are so we pull leads into the middle of our zones as clients.

For example, my mother-in-law had fashion shows whenever she could to attract people to the front of her shop. Think of the local hardware that puts on a BBQ Saturday morning, a bar that puts on live music. The pull effect is about creating a warm environment for people. And the better we create that environment, the more pull effect it has, and the less we need to do to make more sales.

The Magnetic Effect

What is the difference between the pull effect and the magnetic effect? They are very similar, so let me explain how I used them.

Firstly, a magnet has two forces: attractive and repulsive.

Firstly, the repulsive magnetic force of the magnetic is the negative magnetic effect. That's when we try to get two magnets to stick, and they push each other away. In sales, this happens when salespeople get all the systems wrong. Like inappropriate questions at the wrong time, they may interrogate and repulse people and push them away, but that's why you're learning these systems from this book to avoid those accidental repulsive forces.

Then the attractive magnetic force is what sticks two magnets together. Our magnetic sales forces start with the pull effect we have already discussed. That's us pulling people into our environment for buying. But the magnetic effect is better considered the second part of the sale, the after-sale. In other words, what are we doing to retain and get clients to stick around longer as clients?

How do we create a magnetic effect?

A sale doesn't mean business is finished, does it?

After the sale, we have to deliver the product or the service, and we want them to stick around. One of the best things we can do when someone does buy something from us is to finish the transaction and thank them for their business. We congratulate and recognise them for it, even shake their hand, because they've just made a great decision. They've just said "yes" to us, and to something they may have been thinking about buying for a long time. Give them a transition from sale to a client and start to get them to stick.

Say something like, "Well done and great decision, and I thank you, so let's get to work and deliver …". Saying something like that starts the magnetic effect of them sticking as a client. After all, you do appreciate

This is what successful people say, do, and when.

their business, don't you? So let them know you do. It's time for them to stick around as clients.

False Positives

Ever had someone say a movie was great, but then you watched it, and it was only OK?

Ever been served a meal that looked unreal, but it was only OK?

Ever had someone say "Yes", but they really meant no?

Situations like this are called false positives.

A false positive in selling is when someone's saying all the right yes answers, but they're really saying no. We hear yes, yes, yes, and they're acting positive, but the reality is, we know they're not going to buy. Our gut instinct tells us that something is not quite right.

There are signs like cold questions or answers and closed body language. And it takes time and years of experience to recognise false positives quickly. And the better we get at these systems, the sooner we can recognise them. One example I keep talking about is the "how much is it" question, which excites most inexperienced salespeople. They think they have a hot lead, forget all the systems, and close too early. They then wonder what happened to that hot lead, which looked like a hot buyer.

Another false positive is when someone says, "I want it now", and suddenly they turn into this horrible person, the sale becomes one-sided, and their negotiation becomes unreasonable. Even though they've said they want it, they start becoming negative. We have all experienced that. They've tricked us! They've come in with the positives but wanted to manipulate us and give us a hard time. We don't need some clients as they are false positives, which is another Business Judo® story in the book 5 Systems of Successful People.

I know what you are thinking, I showed you Socrates Successful Method to get all our yes answers, and one of the reasons we ask questions is to get a positive, which is still true. So, when unsure if this

This is what successful people say, do, and when.

is a false positive, use a test close. It's one of the three closes we can use, and I will teach these later in the book.

Getting good at avoiding false positives means you will make more sales and make more money.

Retention

Remember the cafe? I wanted to go into the cafe's hot zone, and they let me go. If she had said, "Come sit down and relax. We will be with you shortly", they would have retained me. It's far easier to make a sale from someone who is in and stays in our warm and hot zones. We make more sales and money when we don't let them go.

Let me explain it this way. When we look at the zones side on, it will look something like this. Call it a funnel if you like. And your funnel also represents the journey of clients as they come into your business and go back into the cold at the bottom. It's just that you want more to stay than go. So client retention has to be a deliberate and intentional action. Not a reaction once you start to lose them.

We spend a lot of time at the top of our sales funnel trying to get new clients, don't we? Doing our marketing and making sales in our zones, and rightly so, it takes time. However, I am saying that we also need to look at the zones for client retention. Our client funnel needs to be as narrow as possible at the base. In other words, if we get 100 sales, it's no good if 50 don't stay clients of our business. That would mean that we'd need 50 more to replace them as we only retained 50%. And that is what is called our client churn or retention rate. It's much better if we retain 90% of them and only need to replace 10 of them, and the 50 becomes a 40% increase in clients instead.

This is what successful people say, do, and when.

Let me put it this way, remember, the worst answer we can get in sales is when they don't buy from us but do with the competition. Well, the 2nd worse outcome was when they were a client but left us for our competition. It's not how many sales you make. It's how many clients you keep!

> **It's not how many sales you make. It's how many clients you keep!**

This is what successful people say, do, and when.

SYSTEM 8

Fish Attracting Device (FAD)

Back in April 2008, as a family, I travelled around Australia for six months. South of Perth, Western Australia, we went on a guided tour of Busselton Pier. The tour guide took us to the end of a pier, where we climbed down the stairs and into a glassed underwater viewing area to see huge schools of fish swimming around. The guide said, "This pier is a massive FAD, which meant a fish-attracting device". Instantly I related this to my business, what's my FAD. Immediately I reflected on my own company. In other words, what was I doing in my company to attract the right fish I wanted for my business? And every business needs a Fish Attracting Device FAD.

> **FAD!**
> **The extra deliberate and intentional actions to attract sales and retain clients in your buying environment!**

Some think FAD is their brand or unique selling proposition (USP), and they do form part of an overall business strategy. But a FAD is more than a brand or a USP. Your FAD is the extra deliberate and intentional actions to attract and retain clients in our buying environment.

Let me keep this simple. FADs can be artificial or natural, just like the pier. The pier is an artificial FAD, and so is a sunken ship or marina. Whereas natural ocean FADs are reefs and headlands. In business, for example, a restaurant overlooking the ocean, their view is a natural FAD. But what about a restaurant that does not have a view? They make their FAD, like events and entertainment, to attract people as they don't have a natural one. The weird thing here is that in business, many times, it's the manufactured FADs that work better than the natural FADs. Why? Because of attitude combined with knowing what to do once the fish arrive. A great FAD system is also used to attract the right type of fish we want to catch. Think about the restaurant again. Will the live band be rock, jazz, or a solo guitarist? What fish will it attract? And when we do our FADs right, we create an environment for even more of the right fish, and our FAD becomes part of the business ecosystem that we make.

Another example. Now think of a restaurant strip down a street. That is a created FAD, and then each restaurant has its own FAD to help us choose them. Sometimes we want a sports bar with massive TVs playing, next door one with live music, or the quiet one with nothing. We pick the one we are attracted to, don't we? Which one tonight? Am I looking for fun or romance? Additionally, there is the side business selling wines. Why? Because the restaurant strip is a FAD. Now, think about how car dealers are all in the same area or medical centres sit beside the hospitals. You get the point. Can you see how successful business leverage their FADs? Even if it's not their own.

One of the biggest FAD trends that started late last century is building super-centres and shopping malls. Massive FADs we have all visited. True? These super-centres attract two types of fish: the retailers who want to be a part of that environment and us as consumers. Inside these, they often have a stage and entertainment to attract and keep us there.

This is what successful businesses do. They attract people to their business with a deliberate and intentional FAD. Making FAD part of my sales system simplified and improved everything. Knowing who my avatar client was, meant that all my actions were to attract those to ReNet, and that was independent offices in the real estate industry. For example, one of my FADs for agents was training and support. That's what I knew they needed. So I created training events and invited everyone as a FAD. So your FADs depend a lot on your avatar client. If I were fishing for Marlin, that would be a completely different strategy to fishing for flathead or salmon swimming up a river, wouldn't it?

Some FADs people use to attract clients are podcast interviews and YouTube channels. But create whatever makes you comfortable and have time for. For example, my mother-in-law used fashion parades for her retail fashion shop. But let's say I was an accountant. What could I do to attract fish? Client information nights are fantastic events. Use Business Judo® and invite a speaker who wants to discuss tax benefits or investing. Put on training days to empower the knowledge of potential and existing clients and position us as industry experts. And yes, you could even interview successful people at events and share them on social media as your podcasts or video interviews. All of these are FADs, and they all work. There are so many FAD options you can use.

The point is that successful businesses don't wait for business. They make it by attracting it! Create your FAD!

Smartest FAD Ever

McDonald's! Who likes McDonald's hamburgers? Not many! But who has been to a McDonald's? Almost everybody! And what was their FAD? Ronald McDonald!

McDonald's worked out who made the decisions for families when they wanted to go to dinner and wasn't mum and dad. It's the kids. So they introduced Ronald McDonald. Why? Because whenever it came to choosing where to go for dinner, the kids would say, "can we go to McDonald's"? McDonald's isn't even a proper restaurant, but if the kids are happy, so are Mum and Dad. And Ronald McDonald was a deliberate FAD system to attract families. Now, look at all the extensions of attracting kids with Mum and Dad. McDonald's created extra FADs like kids' parties and playgrounds, colouring-in paper, kids' meals and toys. Hook, line and sinker, people went to McDonald's in droves.

McDonald's is brilliant, I love their systems, and their understanding of FAD is one of the best examples. Even when they opened a restaurant, a requirement was their HUGE golden arches pole, the huge M we see driving down the road. That was a strategy to get us in. They also tried to only ever build on corner blocks. Why? They knew they needed to make it easier for people to get in and out once we saw them. One time, I saw them demolish a successful McDonald's in Broadmeadows Newcastle, only to move it 100 meters away because they wanted to be on a corner block.

Today McDonald's has evolved, and Ronald McDonald is less of a FAD. For some time now, they have been using Business Judo® and leveraging other people's FADs. We now find them in service centres, airports and shopping malls. They changed the seating from fixed to movable chairs (if you're old enough to remember) so people could get comfortable. The latest restaurants even have bar-type settings. They no longer look like kids' restaurants and look more modern, attracting business people to eat and stay. If you were born after the year 2000, you probably don't know what I am talking about, but McDonald's is the successful McDonald's you know today from their continued development of FADs.

One of their latest FADs is the McCafe. McCafe started in Australia in 1993. They saw the emergence of a cafe society. McDonald's clients were being attracted away by a cafe experience and healthier options, not just a burger. So Mcdonald's was not the favourite anymore. And McCafe worked; it met their clients' conditions, actions and needs, and then in 2014, even the USA introduced McCafe, although this new FAD pivot saw the downplay of old Ronald. He still exists but sits in the background, not welcoming people at the front door or inviting the kids in like he did when I was young.

This is what successful people say, do, and when.

Interestingly, McDonald's always tries new burgers and giveaways, but it's not always been their food that has attracted us. So with the new McCafe FAD, comfortable bars and stools were used to attract people back in. And it did.

Our FADs

We are not Mcdonald's, but we should learn a lot from successful businesses like theirs. The most important thing is that a FAD is an essential and deliberate system in your business. When I was selling insurance, we didn't have a FAD, we 100% cold called, and that's just hard work. So with an excellent FAD system, we attract buyers into our buying environment instead of working hard.

What assets do you have naturally, and what can you create artificially to attract sales and clients? Like in retail, the colour the shop is painted, the flags and the 50% off clothes rack out the front. These actions are obvious, but what about putting on a fashion parade, champagne nights, or even a person out the front on a PA system talking? See the difference? Think of the car dealers again. They often use FAD tactics to motivate us to visit their hot zones, like weekend BBQs and demonstration days.

What's your FAD?

What's going to attract people from the cold zone?

What do you need to do in your buying environment to attract people?

Yes, your presentation, brand, colour schemes, and marketing all help. Everything that goes out does attract buyers to your business. Let's consider other cafes or coffee shops if we continue down the McCafe path. Their brand may be hipster, timbered and organic-looking cafes to attract hipster people. Then we see a clean, uncluttered and very hygienic-looking cafe that attracts those people. Remember, FAD is more than a brand. It's the extra deliberate, intentional actions to attract sales and retain clients in your buying environment!

This is what successful people say, do, and when.

SYSTEM 9

Trojan Horse

A Trojan Horse is a system that I caught onto early in business. The Trojan Horse story, in a simplistic view, is about how the Greeks gave a horse as a gift as a tactic to get inside the city of Troy. However, hidden inside the horse were men ready to take the city, and it worked. Now we don't need to understand the correct history and story of the Trojan Horse. We must only understand the opportunity to use this system in our business.

> **Trojan Horse**
> *What tactics can you deploy to have people enter your business, allowing for even more business opportunities?*

Knowing the Trojan Horse system profoundly affected how I thought about products and services in my business. In other words, what tactics can you deploy that allow for even more opportunities?

A Trojan Horse may be something you charge for, or it could even be a **loss leader** product, meaning it could be something we make little or no profit from or even give away for free. For example, have you ever purchased the 30c ice cream from McDonald's? Even if you haven't, you know about them. It was 30c, then 50c, now 70c, and I am sure it will be dearer in the future. So they are not free, but there is no way they make money from the soft-serve ice cream cone, but as a Trojan Horse, it's perfect. People go to get the kids cheap ice cream, and what happens

SELL MORE MAKE MORE - The Best Sales Systems Ever!

more often than not? Yep! The order grows by a few other things too. Very smart. More importantly, people return to McDonald's and their environment, not the competition. McDonald's is very clever, aren't they?

Another example of how I used a Trojan Horse in my business was website design. A website is necessary for every real estate office, so I decided to use that as my Trojan Horse. Like Mcdonald's, we still charged for our work. We often made great money on website design, but profiting from websites was only one of our income streams. The software was. What I really wanted agents to do was buy our real estate software and stay with us for a long time. But I knew every real estate office needed a website, and their salespeople needed one too. Often real estate agents didn't come to us for software, they came because of the things they could see they needed, like a website, so we used Business Judo® and the Trojan Horse system to win.

Let me explain it this way. Website design for ReNet was our Trojan Horse, which meant that when someone came into our environment, and we had our conversation about their website needs, it allowed us to also talk to them about the actual business conversation we needed to have. Which was the software, and the reality was that the website and software only worked together anyway. They couldn't have the website without the software, regardless. They could have the software without a website, but not a website without our software, just the way ReNet worked. So all they knew was that they needed a new website, so we used their website needs as our Trojan Horse.

To do this effectively and cheaply, we developed template websites that we could do either for free or very cheap. They were simple, and we had already built them to suit many agents for their everyday use. Perfect Time Duplication®. The good news was that we still made money every year from website design, but we made more when they became software clients.

Can you think of some businesses and their Trojan Horse systems? Back to the restaurant example again, a Trojan Horse could be their happy hour at the bar, wine-tasting nights, etc. A Trojan Horse is not necessary for a successful business, but it does work, and that's why many successful companies use this system.

World's Best

Successful businesses intentionally use their Trojan Horse system all the time. There have been a few fantastic Trojan Horses. I will use three tech examples we all know about: Microsoft, Apple and Google.

One of the very first things that Microsoft did was collaborate with IBM. IBM was Microsoft's Trojan Horse. IBM needed to make it easier for clients to use their computers, so Microsoft installed their Windows operating system on IBM computers. Sure, Microsoft made money from IBM, but as a Trojan Horse, they made so much more from their other products that everyone needed too. When we purchased a computer with Microsoft operating system installed, we also needed to buy compatible Microsoft Office products, didn't we? Then, by the turn of the century, just about everyone globally had Microsoft products and services on a computer. Talk about a perfect system, a Trojan Horse aligned with perfect Business Judo®.

Apple, Microsoft's competition, is struggling at a distant 2nd to Microsoft. Then in 2001, Apple created this little product called the iPod. You remember the iPod, don't you? The iPod replaced the Sony Walkman, a little digital music player that was much better than the Walkman. Just about everyone had 1, if not 2. I'm sure we had 4. In other words, they managed to create this great little solution to make music mobile, but at the same time, we needed to have Apple software on our Microsoft computers too. We needed iTunes. The best bit, the whole music system worked perfectly and all the time. The iPods were unreal, the music synced, and that's why everyone had one. So Apples Trojan Horse was iTunes, it was free, and we needed it on our computers even if we used Microsoft.

Then people's confidence in Apple solutions and products grew. The iPod was perfect, and iTunes was easy and synced properly every time.

So what started to happen? Through that iPod Trojan Horse experience, people became more confident, and suddenly, people began buying Apple computers too. They were more expensive but reliable, as everything worked all the time, just like the iPod. And that's how Apple started to gain market share from customers who would never have looked at Apple products in the past.

Then, Apple brought out more products and services after the iPod, not just bigger iPods with screens, and they turned the iPod into the iPhone, then iPhone into iPads. See how they did that? And it all started because of their little Trojan Horse. They went from a distant 2nd to Microsoft in tech to become the world's first trillion-dollar company.

Finally, Google, what was googles Trojan Horse? Their search engine! It seems obvious because that's what they are, a search engine. But when they started, they started differently from every other search engine, and then all the others failed. Some of you may remember that in the early days, we had to submit our websites to search engines manually on the internet, just like telling the yellow pages who we were (if you don't know what the yellow pages were, ask your parents). So many needed us to pay to be on their search results too. But Google gave the search results away for free. Now, Google is so mainstream that many have replaced the word 'search' with 'Google it', even when they are not using Google. Google has become a household name.

The funny story here is that when I started ReNet, and I was talking to real estate agents about their website being found on the internet via Google, many needed to learn who or what Google was. The most common response I got was, "What's Google"? "Who would go to that website"? Yep, it was not easy in the early days of the Internet. Not only did we have to sell people new technology, but we also had to educate them too. People say it was easy in the early days of the Internet, but it wasn't. I had to use every sales system I could to change people's perspectives and get them to adapt to the future and my software.

The Trojan Horse system works. I used it, these companies use it, and many successful businesses do. So how can you use it?

This is what successful people say, do, and when.

In Our Business

OK, so we're not Microsoft, Apple or Google. We may not be a million, billion or trillion-dollar company (yet). But I suggest you can use a Trojan Horse to your advantage. I created websites to use as my standard Trojan Horse, but I also used training events, XML data distribution, and other industry solutions, and they worked brilliantly! Talk about working smarter rather than harder! Or getting paid more and doing less! But let's look at some classic examples I know you'll know.

So for all the ladies, whenever you walk into a department store, how often is someone at the front to greet you with samples? They are more than happy to show you how to use them. What are they doing? They're Trojan Horsing you! It's a Trojan Horse for the conversation AND the products. It's the chance to give you a product sample and get a few minutes of your time. And they have been using this system forever and will continue. Why? It works!

For car buyers, some dealers give a free car wash away as a lifetime offer. What a bargain, but what are they doing? They are Trojan-horsing us. They want us to return to their business now and then, so we see what's new. They want us to come back into their hot zone, into their buying environment occasionally, hoping we buy from them again and don't buy elsewhere. It's not a free car wash. It's a Trojan Horse system for the retention of clients.

Some people call this system a loss leader, a freemium offer, discounts, special offers, offers as a call to action, and that's OK too. In other words, giving something is OK to get in the door. So a Trojan Horse can be many things, and just like big business, you can make money out of them too. It does not have to be free!

But here's another example I had recently. Once, I was speaking at a conference, and another person there had a book. It was just a little book, nice and easy to read. I had to look through it, and it was a great book. But what did this person really do? They weren't an author. They conducted courses about writing books and coaching people. That was

This is what successful people say, do, and when.

their actual business, not the book. The book was their business card in a glorified way. In other words, the book was their Trojan Horse.

Using a Trojan Horse

There are two sides to the Trojan Horse, and it's not just about giving away products for free. A Trojan Horse is used to get more sales. So what can you use in your business right now? Think back to the cold and warm zones. What can you do?

Make a list of all your products and services. What are some of the things that you know that everyone wants or needs? Like selling lollies to kids. We know that when we get the kids into our shop for the lollies, their parents buy something too. It doesn't mean we gave the lollies away for free. Does it?

Trojan Horse doesn't have to be something we give away for free. So don't confuse free as a Trojan Horse. That's different from how it works. It can be free, or you may break even, but the best Trojan horses are the profitable ones.

When you list all your products and services, look at what's one of the shiniest, most attractive business offers you know everyone likes and wants. What attracts the most amount of people? Then, what can you give as either a value add, loss leader or a way of attracting people to your business so you can sell more?

Every business needs to have a Trojan Horse, So work out what it is in your business and then use it to your advantage to grow your business.

SYSTEM 10

Using Brochures

I get this all the time "But Scotty, I am working so hard, I am handing out my brochures and business cards, but I'm not making any money".

There is a good reason for that, and I understand why salespeople think a brochure will sell. They are full of information and pretty pictures, and most people have invested so much energy, time and money in making their brochures look unreal. But brochures don't sell!

I see people who are new to sales, and they get their brochures, business cards, and website ready, let's call it their marketing material. They then think sales will start coming in, believing people will look at these and buy. And while that can happen, selling is not that easy, or else that's all we would need to do, and we'd all have marketing material and no need for a salesperson, would there?

But we are the salespeople, not our marketing material. Because marketing material does not sell as it can not have the same quality conversation we can, can it?

Yes, it's common for buyers to ask for them too. "But Scotty, people ask for them all the time". Of course, they do! But why? Because they want to get rid of us. They ask, "Have you got a brochure"? And we hear, "Can we buy" but that's not the case. "Have you got a brochure"? That's secret buyer's code for "I'll take the brochure and never call you back"! Think about it, they rarely call back, do they?

Your brochure can explain features, advantages and benefits, and many look fantastic. But the number one reason not to use brochures and business cards for selling is that once we give them out, we also give out control. In other words, it's the same as letting them go into the cold zone or "You get back to me". A typical response from someone with a brochure is when you phone them to see what they think is, "I have your brochure, and I will get back to you once I take a look", but they rarely do. And then what do we do? It's hard to come back from that. Isn't it? Some tell me they have had people phone and buy from their business cards or brochures. And I agree, it does happen, but the strike rate is really low or only suitable for those leads who are hot buyers or right up the top of the Business of Thirds®. For the rest of the zones, it's a terrible strike rate.

So what's the best tactic for marketing material?

Great questions. Just so that you know. Business cards and brochures were not part of the system for selling insurance, nor ReNet. So save your money and do more sales training and develop a salesperson attitude instead.

OK, I know that's not how most people think, so if you must, let's use them better then. So if you want my opinion, get rid of them unless you use them to generate more questions rather than give answers. Nonetheless, let's look at them if you must.

Brochures do not sell!

I don't have business cards, and they are easy to eliminate for your sales system! But do collect them from leads. That's better than giving them yours. You don't even need to exchange them. What I do is I get their details and schedule what's next with a plan or mud map instead. After all, that's what I wanted a card to do, so skip the card and do it now! That also means that I am in control of my environment, and I haven't let them go back into the cold zone, and I help them enter my

This is what successful people say, do, and when.

warm zones. See how that's a better system? It's quicker and has a better strike rate. Try it. It works!

And what's the best tactic for brochures? For example, I have coached many people. Some have been in the print industry and struggling to sell advertising in their magazines. They show me their beautiful pricing brochure, yet can't understand why more people are not buying from it when they leave it with them. Can you see what is happening? Why aren't more people buying from their pricing brochure when they leave it with leads? Because people don't buy from brochures! But they are actually in a perfect position, as they can use their magazine as their brochure and presentation prop rather than the pricing brochure. But because they are in the print industry, they are addicted to creating print material, and they are cheap for them to make. So I teach them to eliminate their pricing brochure and use the real thing, the magazine publication, in their conversation instead of leaving a pricing brochure. It has perfect examples for the lead, and leads can touch and see it for real. The real thing also has perfect inference (more on inference later) for the lead to buy. A bit like sitting in a car or test-driving it. It's way better than a brochure, hey?

Sometimes a brochure has a great call to action, a discount, etc. But that's selling on price. So fair enough. But I want you to make more sales and make more money. And if you're always discounting the price, that's NOT how you make more money. It just makes you busy.

If you want to see great salespeople at work, go to the local Sunday markets, where you find people selling their products passionately from the boot of their cars. Why? If they don't sell it, they must pack it back up and go home without any money. So they are hungry. They know their stuff, operate on small budgets, and tend to do very well with their sales approach. But one day, I went up to a guy selling leather belts, and the first thing he did was give me his brochure, then told me if I wanted to know more, I could go to his website. I was right there, in his hot zone, and he gave me all the reasons to walk away, yet he thought he had done well, but he totally missed the point. Not sure who trained him, but he must lose many sales because of his system of seeing how

This is what successful people say, do, and when.

many brochures he could give out. Maybe he had some sales from his brochure one day, so now he thinks this is a perfect system. Can you see how this goes against every system in this book?

Nonetheless, if you use brochures or business cards, I want you to get the most out of them. So let's work on using them to have that positive magnetic effect rather than a push effect. Let's work through how to use them if you must.

Our Objective

There is a time and place for everything, including brochures. But you must know the objective of your brochure. For example, if I was a local pizza shop and Tuesday nights were quiet nights, and I wanted to do a run of flyers around the local community saying $5 pizza night to attract business (think Trojan Horse), then a brochure may be perfect. A brochure here could have an excellent pull effect on people, bringing them into my hot zone. But note that it's easy because it sells at a discounted price.

By the way, when I was a teenager, one of the jobs I cold-called for and successfully got was letterbox drops for the local roast chicken shop. They paid me $0.02 for each flyer for me to do their drops. They kept paying me to do it because they must have worked for them.

So what is the objective of your brochure? When ReNet was required to have brochures, which was very rare, such as attendee bags at conferences. Some attendees were already clients, and the others were getting handed out so much noise in printed material that anything I did was just more noise. So my objective then was to quickly reinforce our products and services and be there for conversation. It's a habit for people to walk up and ask for a brochure from the exhibition stands, so we entertained it. But what was my objective? Not to give away brochures. So our brochures were just pretty pictures as examples. They were only there to start the conversation. I also didn't want to say no to anyone, and it was expected behaviour at conferences, so I only wanted

This is what successful people say, do, and when.

to get their details for following up with a scheduled call, not give a brochure.

People believe brochures are for selling, and they can open people's minds. They may even have a place for the pull effect and the people in the cold zone. But to give control to someone in the warm zone means we are almost signing off on our ability to control our buying environment. They now have our information, and they have control. Once that happens, it's hard to get back!

For example, when walking in the shopping mall, someone uses their Trojan Horse to get your attention with a sample and says, "Hello, how are you"? Generally, we either ignore them or take the sample and say something to get away as fast as possible, don't we? But then, they try to engage in conversation using the sample to pull us in. They are good at it, aren't they?

That's the same psychology of the person we're giving our brochure to. Do they want to buy it? Probably not! I know that 99 times out of 100, they're going take our brochure so they can say, "I'll get back to you". What can we do then? We are buggered. I learnt that we have physically given them control over what's next. When someone gets my attention in the mall with a sample, I say, "Thanks, I will try it," and keep walking even if I am uninterested. I want to be nice to them, then throw it in the bin around the corner. We have all done this, haven't we? It's so easy, "Can I take your business card or brochure"? We ask for it so we can leave without someone selling us something.

On the other hand, if we're prospecting and this is a one-on-one presentation with someone, then a brochure may be used as a presentation prop, just like those in the mall. It's a reference and talking point. And just like a salesperson in the mall, you do the selling and don't expect the brochure to sell for you. That's your job. But if you want to be like the people in the mall and use one, then use it as a presentation prop, just like many of them do. Their sales training is excellent, and you can learn a lot from them too.

Give and Take

Yep, think, give and take. If you are going to share something, you want to get something back in return. Like their details!

Remember, just like the salespeople in the mall. Know precisely what you are trying to do during your brochure handover and practice and train for it. So next time you are at an event or conference, you will know precisely what you will do and say. We really want an introduction or presentation from our brochure or business cards, don't we? So during the handover, have a plan of action for them and try to get a genuine reason for your follow-up. Anyone genuinely interested will willingly give you their contact details, so don't be afraid to ask for them. And it's professional to do so.

When someone was interested in our products and asks for a brochure, we think it's them asking, "Why you? Can you help me"? So, yep, we assumed that when someone asked for a handout, they were saying, "Can you tell me more information"? And when we go in with that mindset, we didn't just hand out brochures.

So we took their details, a name and phone number. So what?

Now ask, "I'll call you next week, and your best time is"? That will qualify them straight away! If they return with "that'd be great," we have a qualified lead. In this case, we make sure that we maintain control. Maybe then ask, "Is Tuesday or Thursday at 2 pm OK for you"? In other words, the conversation is not about the brochure. It's about what's next in our buying environment.

I still prefer not to produce or give brochures because they cost money yet do very little. The example above can be achieved without the need for a handout.

Next, we must avoid this response when we follow up with them, "I've got your brochure and phone number, so I'll get back to you".

Remember earlier, with the 3 parts to a transaction? This is where that strong close comes into play from the previous conversation. We want them to be expecting our call and welcome us. And by properly closing the last discussion, I don't mean your "thank you". I mean that you have sowed the seeds and the reason for your call. When we hand out a brochure (or not), we repeat back to them their hot spot, pain, or need. Repeat it and say how much you look forward to sharing some solutions with them. For example, if someone asked for a brochure on website design, and they mentioned that there's was getting old, repeat something back to them like this "I look forward to catching up Tuesday, and I will prepare some examples of new modern websites for you to look at". You can see how that is more effective than "Talk Tuesday" or "Thank you". The closing of your conversation makes a massive difference to when you make your follow-up phone call next.

And finally, if your brochure is for a one-on-one, then it's perfect as a prop, and when someone asks, "Have you got a brochure", rather than let them take control of the brochure, immediately start to use it in conversation as a prop right then. What I am saying is this! Do not physically give it to them yet! Hold it out front in presentation mode! Show them the information on the brochure first and make a couple of quick FAB statements so you get a positive response. That means you will know their interest level based on the 4 Levels of the Human Mind and what buying zone they are in for the next stage in your sales cycle.

Following Up

Firstly, don't be offended that 99.9% of people will not call you back from your brochure or business card. So what is the best practice here? Forget about brochures and business cards! You don't need them. OK, I won't bring this up again, as you may have excellent marketing materials. But think like this, it's not really important what's on them, as you only need them to get their phone number or an appointment anyway. Then when you do our follow-up, you start the whole sales system again, except that maybe they are now in your warm zone or even a warm lead.

Let me give a typical example. Let's say I was at an event and handed out brochures. I get a phone number from Paul and phone him, and then I say, "Hi Paul, it's Scott here; I gave you the brochure when we

This is what successful people say, do, and when.

met at XYZ". As if the brochure is important, but it's not! But don't even mention it, trust me. It would be best to forget about the brochure, as it was only a tactic to get here, to have a conversation. The brochure has done its job.

Let me give a better example. "Hi Paul, it's Scott here, we met at XYZ, and I have some good news. I have done some research and have some great ideas that I believe will interest you also". See how this example ignores the brochure. It's much better to talk about what's important and your solutions. In other words, if you talk about the brochure, you are bringing up their exit strategy again, which is the last thing you want to do! The brochure doesn't sell. You do!

So the best system is to think of this as a warm call and remember what you said when you gave that brochure. How did you close that transaction so you can segway that as your introduction here? For example, "Hi Paul, We were talking last week at the conference, and you asked about modernising your website. I have a few examples I believe will interest you also". See the difference? If you can't remember, you will need to think of something. But either way, forgetting about the brochure is the best practice.

This system avoids the response, "I have your brochure. I'll get back to you if I am interested". Because once we hear that, they are lost! Maybe they were interested, but now they are not, and it's tough to warm them back up again from here. So they are out in the cold now, and you must let them go.

Something to think about is this. Many people also send emails as quotes full of information and pricing. They have simply replaced the brochure with an email. But the same rule applies. When someone asks, "Can you email me some information" it sounds hot. So we better send them some info so they can reply and say, "I'll buy it". But why don't they? Emails are modern brochures, and they don't sell either. We do!

So when someone asks me for an email with more information, I pick up the phone and talk to them, and I do not email them as my first reply. "Can you email me" is the same as when someone asks, "How

This is what successful people say, do, and when.

much is it"? They are really asking for more information. That's why I pick up the phone and have a conversation as my first response to everything. Also, when I send an email, it may have information but rarely a price. The email needs to raise as many questions as possible until the next time we talk. Then the plan is to schedule an appointment for a good time to talk. I am the salesperson, and I need them to know what my solution is, and a brochure or email does not respond to their needs as I can when I am talking to someone in person. Maybe for smaller transactions, it's OK, but for larger transactions, our response is every part of creating an environment for people to buy.

Brochures, emails and business cards do not sell. We do!

SYSTEM 11

Involving People

My wife once sent me to the local French Patisserie to get 2 French sticks. I asked the girl behind the counter, "Can I have two long French sticks, please".

She politely said… "Sorry. We don't have any Baguettes left"!

I looked at the piece of paper with my shopping list, and it didn't say Baguettes. My wife's instructions were clear, French sticks.

So I asked again…. "My wife has asked for two long French sticks".

And she repeated… "Sorry. We don't have any Baguettes left"!

Now, not being stupid. I learned quickly that French sticks and Baguettes must be the same things. It's just that I felt stupid for not knowing. It was more important that they were correct than helping me.

There was a better way to handle me as a mere male. But I walked out, told my wife and friends, and we haven't been back. I have now learnt my lesson about French sticks and Baguettes. But they lost respect and clients.

Generally, clients come to us so we can help them make a buying decision. We go to an accountant for expert accounting advice, a solicitor for specialist legal advice, a builder for expert building advice, etc. Regardless of what we do, we want to feel appreciated and that we are, as buyers, getting looked after and valued, and not a problem to them. It sounds simple enough, but how do we do it? What's the system?

This is what successful people say, do, and when.

Tell Me, Show Me, Involve Me

Tell me, I'll forget!

Show me, I may remember!

Involve me, and I'll understand.

So how do we involve people in our conversations?

Using a car yard as an example, we sit in the car or even take it for a test drive. That was easy, hey? But there is more we can do if we are car salespeople. Let me explain. Imagine a guy comes in. He's a builder and wants to buy a new work truck. He would probably start talking, saying things like, "I'm thinking about buying a new work truck". So to involve him, the best thing we can do right now is to let him talk, listen to what he needs, and then engage with him. And letting him speak and being involved in buying a new truck allows him to tell us why he needs it.

As a salesperson, we create an environment for him to buy simply by listening and being engaged, not by telling or showing but by involving him. Then eventually, as we listen, he tells us ALL the information we will need as he describes to us his why. The moment he starts talking about himself, that's the perfect opportunity to get involved, stop, listen, and engage in whatever he says. So rather than just telling them all about the car and showing why he should buy from us, ask him questions about what he knows the most about, that's him. As he comments, get him to explain it more, and every time he does, he does his own Socrates Successful Method on himself, and that's perfect Business Judo®.

Suddenly, we are both involved in his conversations as he buys. And being involved can be as easy as that.

The point is that there's only one reason someone comes to talk to you about your products and services. It's because they're interested in them. They think you may provide a solution for them, so let them be involved and tell you why they want yours.

The builder came into the car yard to buy a truck, not a motorbike. So as a salesperson, we let them involve themselves in their conversations about what it is they want and all the reasons why. And letting them be involved is much easier than asking many useless questions. Isn't it?

So if we're talking more than them, we're probably telling rather than engaging. If we're presenting to them and not listening to their questions, we're showing and telling, not involving.

So by involving them to talk about themselves, their business, what they want to do, and their reasons, we also get to know their why. For example, we would like to know why they want to buy. So involving people is more than getting them to test drive. But first, we need to get involved in the conversation about them.

It's easy to forget this because we're selling and presenting. As salespeople, selling means we have to be telling everyone everything. But we don't! What we need to do is involve people in everything. And you don't need to talk or sell. Simply listening and being involved will help you make more sales and make more money.

2 Ears, 1 Mouth

This is a great system to remember about listening; you have two ears and one mouth and must use them accordingly.

> **We have 2 ears and 1 mouth, use them accordingly!**

As I have said a few times now, if we're doing more talking than the buyer, then we're doing more selling than they're doing buying. So once a buyer starts talking about their hot spots, problems or needs, let them

This is what successful people say, do, and when.

talk. We even ask questions about what they are talking about. Simple hey? This is perfect Business Judo® because the buyer is now telling us the answers. They give us their information as we let them engage with themselves and be involved in our products.

Obviously, with a pizza shop or a business with many small transactional items, this may not be as important as when selling big-ticket products and services, but involving someone at every price level matters.

Involving someone could even be like teaching someone. Let's use the car dealer again, I'm buying a new car, and the salesman sits me in the passenger seat and tells me or shows me what all the buttons do. But to involve me, it would be better to let me press all the buttons, listen to my questions, and then answer them. Or, like in a fashion store, they are engaged in the buying process when clothes are tried on. So, for example, when I sold ReNet, I did the presentation on the office computer and got them to press the keyboard to make it work. I got them involved in how easy it was. And that's why it was like selling lollies to kids because they were involved and engaged.

At the end of the day, involving buyers is as simple as giving them some options and making them feel that there is a solution. Just like letting someone sit down at the cafe while they finish putting the chairs out and warm up the coffee machine.

To go back to the car dealer example. I once walked into a car dealer with a surfboard, as I wanted to make sure it fitted into the cars I was considering buying. So talk about easy prey for a car salesperson. I was easy to get involved with as I had a surfboard and was putting it into cars to test if it fitted! And most people want to be involved, and we must let them. That's why they came to us first. Isn't it?

Possession is 9/10th of the Law

Have you ever heard the saying "possession is 9/10th of the law"? Well, it's true when it comes to sales. But how do we create possession in sales to get involvement?

This is what successful people say, do, and when.

SELL MORE MAKE MORE - The Best Sales Systems Ever!

If you have kids, have you ever walked into the pet store and then let the kids hold the baby pets? While it's a great way to spend an hour, it's also tough for the kids to put them back into their cages. "But can't we take a puppy home"? And that's how many pets are bought because of possession. Who wants to give a puppy back? Not the kids!

Remember when I walked up to the cafe, and they said they were not open yet? Well, this is the system they could have used. They could have sat me down, said they wouldn't be long, and given me a glass of water. That's possession! As once I am sitting down, it's more likely that I will stay, order, and not leave.

Let's go back to the Ford dealer; you may recall that a hot zone was test-driving a car. Yep, that's also possession. Customers get to drive the vehicle, and when they like how it goes and the smell of a new car, they get a feeling of ownership. They feel great, and if the salesperson is good to them, there is more chance that someone will buy after a good test drive. And that's why car salespeople try to get us to test drive a car. Because that's when we start to buy it, own it, and feel the vehicle. That's possession!

We can also **Speak it!** Possession means talking as if they already own it and are already customers. The puppy or your puppy. The car or your car. The car comes in a range of colours, or your car comes in a range of colours. See the difference? Talking you and yours, that's possession.

Let me give an example of how I started ReNet with only a few customers. When I went into a real estate agent's office, I deliberately did two things to create possession. Firstly I would populate their software as if it was already theirs, with some of their properties for sale, staff, and branded with their logos. I would invest this time before I walked into their business completely cold. So when they looked at the software, it was already as if it was theirs. The paradigm shift for them was that I was presenting their software to them, not my software. "Here are your properties on your software". See the paradigm shift I used? I gave them possession of the software, and although they didn't know me or ReNet, the software already had their properties, staff and branding. That's possession.

Secondly, I got the staff to drive the software while presenting. In other words, I didn't show them how to upload a photo or change a price, and I got them to do it themselves. That's how they knew the software would save them time, and they loved it. That's possession. And Using a possession system is perfect Business Judo® too, and for my software, it became like selling lollies to kids. My stake rate was 1 in 2. Yep, for every second presentation I did, I made a sale. In 2003 I was making $1,000+ in the morning and $1,000+ in the afternoon.

So how do fashion retailers use this system? Their change rooms. They always want to know if we're going to try something on, don't they? Because they know if we see ourselves in something nice, there is more chance we will buy it regardless of the price. True? That's also why many software companies now give free trials because that's just like trying on clothes. That's possession.

Think 'touch and feel', especially if you've got a product. Once you hand something to somebody, and they start playing with it and like it, then chances are higher that they may want to buy it.

So how do we use possession without a product, such as a service?

We must practice talking more about them already being users or owners. In other words, rather than "when you buy this", it's "when you use this". See the difference? One statement is selling, and the other is possession. Possession is 9/10ths of the law in sales.

For example, when training people in sales one-on-one, I often inspect the last few emails they have sent. That tells me a lot about how they think and what training they have had, and it's incredible how often the emails are about them, not the lead. Sometimes the emails contain a job quote, which I am not a fan of. That aside, the quote is not made to look like the customers own it or take them on a visual journey of what will happen next. Often, none or very little possession is used in these emails or job quotes. But possession can be as simple as adding a splash of customer branding or colours to the quote. So simple to implement, and the impact is enormous on the person receiving the email or quote.

Our job is to always think about systems where customers feel ownership of the product and as customers before they even are. That's possession!

B2B

Wouldn't it be great to have products and services and people just pay for them? We build, and they buy, and we make as much money as we want. Wouldn't that be a perfect world? I've often joked that if I just got rid of all the customers and kept all the profits, that business would be fantastic! Wouldn't it? But that wasn't my reality, and I imagine it's not yours either. Without customers, there's no income, which means no profit, and no profit, then there's no business.

So what's B2B in sales? Most people think that means Business-to-Business, and yes, it still does. But when it comes to B2B as a system, it doesn't! Remember the previous systems discussing things like questions, possession, and involvement? Well, as a system, B2B means Belly-to-Belly (face-to-face). When I sold insurance and was a commission-only salesperson, we had to get off our bums and talk to people, go and have conversations Belly-to-Belly It was the only way we could get paid. Sales were never coming to us. We had to find them.

Today we can use technology to have Belly-to-Belly too. Like video calls with people from anywhere in the world. So it's even more accessible than ever to have sales conversations with others.

So why is Belly-to-Belly (face-to-face) so important? Remember, there are two things people buy: the product and us. If people know, like and trust the product, they may purchase it regardless of us. But a sale is imminent when they know, like and trust both the product and us. True? Remember I walked into a car yard with a surfboard? I still bought a ute, but not that day! I spent my money with somebody else as nobody served me. True story.

What's the best and most effective way you build know, like, and trust? Belly-to-Belly. Actually talking to people.

I bet you have walked into a retail store and not been served. You walked around, were keen to buy but didn't feel the love and walked out. We all have! Because the store doesn't understand B2B. Sometimes that is their business model. Like the massive hardware stores you visit, they sell on price but with little or no service. If I wanted service from a hardware store, I would go to the smaller run hardware to ask them questions. And I bet you've done that before too. It might cost more, but we get service, and the bit extra it costs is saved by the problems being solved the first time. That's B2B. People really want us to engage with them, just like we want when we're buying too.

To reverse Belly-to-Belly, business cards, brochures, emails, websites, social media, etc., they can not sell as well as you, can they? While it's great when people buy with little input, most prefer to purchase from you and your expertise. So let them.

B2B should be face-to-face in a physical location, but the good news is that there are many ways you can make B2B happen without it. Simple tactics like picking up the phone and talking to someone rather than replying by email to enquiries. I've seen people on social media ask a buying question, and the person responded on the chat with an answer and then said, "Let me know if you have any more questions". That person does not understand B2B, do they? With B2B, we talk to people and start our Belly-to-Belly, face-to-face conversations regardless of a physical location or not.

Engaging directly with leads, Belly-2-Belly quickly builds know, like, and trust, the confidence and belief that you are the right person with the right products to buy from.

Retention

When is the best time to sell a man a tie? When they have purchased a suit. And it's much easier to sell something to someone who has already purchased from us. And even if our products are not renewable,

This is what successful people say, do, and when.

having clients return for more is retention. I mean, we don't want them to buy from someone else next time, do we?

We can do nice things like picking up the phone and asking how it's going, talking about new products and getting them involved, or even a survey on what they would like next. Another excellent way of retention nowadays is starting a podcast and getting them as guests on it or case studies, blogs and articles on your websites. All perfect Business Judo® too. We're promoting a client and all the good things they are doing and giving us some marketing exposure.

Getting testimonials from clients too, and when they talk about their positive experiences, they also reinforce to themselves what the positive experience is for them as a client.

Plan retention as part of the sales cycle, as you want them to continue to be clients. So, you start the retention plan early. And the bigger the sale, the more you need to involve customers in your future for retention.

Client retention should not be an afterthought.

Deliberate Mistakes

We all appreciate an expert, don't we?

But what we appreciate even more than an expert is when that expert involves us in a solution we want, don't we?

For example, I was told of a builder that used this deliberate mistakes system to win business. One day this builder was running late for his appointment to quote a job, so he phoned the customer and let them know he would be 15 minutes late. But when he did his presentation and quote and won their business, the client told him it was because he had excellent communication skills by calling them when running late. Therefore, what he thought he would do as part of his sales systems was more deliberate mistakes and always run late and phone the client to win over their confidence. It worked once, so why not keep making this deliberate mistake and win every job? But what really won him the

This is what successful people say, do, and when.

business? It was not him running late, was it? It was his communication and involvement. He could have used the same technique about being on time or even running early, couldn't he? There are better ways to make positive, deliberate mistakes.

Back in the 90s, we had a full word-for-word sales script we followed, and it worked! But we got so good at delivering the scripts that we started to sound like a real-life infomercial (LOL). So I introduced deliberate mistakes to break up my presentations. Simple techniques like deliberately pausing and fumbling and stumbling. Because I needed this presentation to be seen as a personal presentation just for them, something other than what I had said 20 times that day.

For example, when there was an interruption to my presentation like a phone call or a customer walked in. I would start the conversation again with, "Now, where was I"? I knew where I was, but this question involved them in what was next. I also paused way more than I needed to so they saw I was thinking about their question. Even though I knew the answer already, I understood the environment, and it was vital that they felt I was personally talking to them.

When I started ReNet, it was a little different, the sale was much larger, and even more involvement was required. So I used lines like, "Let me check that for you" or "Let me have a look for you". Even though I know the answer, I don't have to have all the answers straight away, do I? We can engage people in conversation by using deliberate mistakes. In other words, they want us to be experts. They also want us to help them and to be human. People don't care how much you know. They want to know how much you care. So having to find out more information for them is a great tactic that shows you care.

Let's use the Ford dealer. They may know how many cars are in stock and what the next delivery has too. But not knowing when asked gives them the perfect deliberate mistake. For example. "Do you have a red one coming into stock"? They could replay with something like, "I'd need to check. Let me check for you"? That's as simple as deliberate mistakes, and involvement needs to be. The double benefit here is that

This is what successful people say, do, and when.

they would also go to the hot zone to check, that's the salesperson's desk.

Sometimes someone can get so bloody good at their presentation that it sounds too good to be true. It's too polished. When we see that, we sometimes think that we don't trust this person as they are just too polished and it seems fake.

So it's OK to be yourself. It's okay when we fumble and stumble. It's OK if we have an odd spelling mistake (I've seen professors make them). I love it when people interact with me and tell me I've made a mistake. That gives me a chance to thank someone for something I do genuinely appreciate.

Today, I am comfortable with having some mistakes in my presentations. A little secret is that sometimes when people see me make a mistake, I mean it to be there! I WANT TO BE ME because I don't want to look too polished in my presentations.

Then the good news is that when we make genuine mistakes, we already know how to bounce and recover because we have been deliberately making small ones already.

Deliberate mistakes are a perfect system for involving clients. It gives them a chance to become involved and share what they know. A perfect way of building up your buying environment.

This is what successful people say, do, and when.

SYSTEM 12

Body Language

If only we knew what buyers were thinking! The good news is that we can, and that's by their body language.

This chapter is an elevated or helicopter view of body language, there are plenty of ways to become an expert, and selling is one of them. What you will learn with this system is how to use it to your advantage. And as with everything in these systems, there are two sides meaning there's their body language and our body language.

On the downside, someone with basic body language knowledge can misread it, as in false positives and negatives. For example, we start talking to someone, and then they cross their arms. That can mean they are closed-minded, that they are cold, or it can even mean they are deep in thought. So body language requires multiple signs to align to be true. As a rule of thumb, three signs. For example, crossed arms, looking away, and not smiling all seem very negative, and it is, so we have to find a way to open them if we want a transaction. Think about the negative body language you give someone in the mall when they try to get your attention. You look down or away from them, and you try your best not to make eye contact when they try their best to get you to look at them.

On the other hand, when a lead is asking questions, what's their body language? Their open arms, facing us, and direct eye contact looks engaging, which means we are in a great position to get a successful transaction. Better still, if they engage and involve themselves with and touch the products (think car dealership). When someone asks questions, their body language is generally positive and reflects that they're in the buying mood. It only closes off if they don't like our answers. So if we see a negative reaction, respond by asking a positive question to make them comfortable again. But don't overthink it, though learning about body language made a huge difference for me. I studied and trained it as an essential sales system. Remember that selling is action and reaction; body language reactions tell you what to do next.

In reverse, when someone starts talking to us, they read us as they engage with us. Are you open and supportive? Are you making eye contact? Do you face your leads when talking to them? Do you look at the products when you explain them? Do you listen attentively? Is there a smile on your face and in your voice?

Your body language is as important as your product presentation. So let's look at a few systems to add to your knowledge.

The Mirror Effect

The mirror effect or mirroring is when we mirror or reflect back what leads, prospects and buyers wear, do, and say.

What we wear. When prospecting and selling insurance to tradespeople on building sites, I would dress similarly to them. Such as wearing boots and not pointy dress shoes. I would not wear a suit and tie, as that's not what they wear. Worse than that, inspectors are the only people wearing formal clothes on a building site. I didn't want them to relate to me as one of them, did I? We mirror our clothes to what makes people feel comfortable talking to us. We need the tradespeople not to think we are from the tax department and avoid us instead. If they come to see us, we wear whatever they expect us to wear.

Think of a retail shop. They wear the clothes they sell. Professionals wear suits, tradespersons in tradies clothes, what are people expecting you to wear?

Eye contact. Mirroring our eye contact and where to look is an advanced technique. Most people mirror where we look when we are talking to them. When we want them to focus on something, we can break eye contact and look at the product or prop, and they will too. If

This is what successful people say, do, and when.

we have a product or prop, position it in front of them, not us. We already know all about it, so make sure it is easy for them to see and engage in it and that it's right in front of them. When we get shoulder to should and direct our eyes and body towards the product or prop, they will mirror us and follow it every time. It's incredible how much power we have with our eyes alone. Then when we want or need to have eye contact, we square up and make eye contact again.

Making people feel comfortable in a buying environment also means mirroring what makes them comfortable. If they are standing, we stand. If they are sitting, we sit. Mirror how they are sitting too. Then if they have a cup of coffee/tea/water, we have a cup of coffee/tea/water too. Making people feel comfortable in the buying environment also means they must know, like and trust us. And people trust people like them, don't they? So mirroring is the deliberate action of being like them.

Directing a Prospects Mind

When someone says to us, "Don't look, but over there is..." what's the first thing we do or want to do? Look, don't we?

I am sure you know that when we talk to someone and look at something else, people wonder what we are looking at and why, so they look too. Don't they? This is 101 in body language and control.

So with our presentations, we can use statements like "look here" when we want to show them something. And if we want them to follow us, use "let me show you something over here", and they will follow. Action and reaction, this tactic is essential as when we're selling, there are times when we need to show something, and we need their full attention. So say and do what you want them to do. And they should mirror you too.

Stop Talking

What if I told you there was a guaranteed way to get a lead to ask questions? Something that works 100% of the time. Would you believe me?

So how do you get people to engage and ask questions? Stop talking!

What happens when we stop talking during a sales presentation?

What's my body language saying? It's your turn now!

Yep, my body language says it's their turn to talk. That's how we get them involved again and ask more questions, which works every single time. To do this properly, we stop talking, square up to them, and look them in the eye in silence. This works perfectly with Socrates Successful Method (earlier in the book). You've made positive statements and finished saying what you want, so it's their turn to talk. So stop.

> **How do we get people to engage and ask questions?**
> **Stop talking!**

And when you stop talking, just like magic, they will say something, which happens 100% of the time. Yep, it never fails. They will ask questions because you've made eye contact and gone silent. Their auto reaction is to want to react/respond. That's a very natural and perfect reaction that happens to 100% of people 100% of the time. Trust me.

Try it! Try talking to someone about something, then look at them and say nothing., then watch them say something. It's like magic.

Positive Language

Have you ever had an email or text message taken out of context? We all have, haven't we? Of course, we didn't mean it, but someone thought something different to what we were thinking. Body language is the physical body, such as our arms, eyes, and legs, and what we say and extend to our words. This is how people react when they hear us talk.

As an example of positive language. Here is a perfect opportunity for a "thank you" and to make someone feel valued. How often do we hear or have we said, "Sorry to keep you"? When we could say "thank you for waiting/holding" and have people feel appreciated.

Our language has to be positive. In other words, when we're having a conversation, it's about what people can do and what they can achieve. Not what they can't. It seems simple, right? However, real-world evidence shows us that this system can be improved in our communication, especially sales.

Generally, we talk about all the positive things we do, but some people accidentally get caught up in negative words. For example, can't, shouldn't, or don't. There may be a place for them, but it's only a tiny percentage of the time. I hear you thinking that you sometimes have to use it when people ask what things you can and can't do. But try not to use the negative. Often, there is a better way to say it with positive words.

Sometimes a negative does add weight to what we're talking about. For example, we may say something like, "We don't want that, do we"? That can flip a negative into a positive. But be careful. When you use it to reinforce the negative, you must follow it with a positive. There must be a positive follow-on after the use of a negative.

The better system is replacing all negative words with positive ones and rephrasing sentences to use all positive ones instead.

Words you may replace…

Can't = Can.

Don't = Do.

Sorry = Thank you.

Bad = Good.

A great habit is writing an email, reading it, finding every negative word, and then replacing it with a positive one. For example, someone would ask, "Can you build a $10,000 website for only $8,000"? We could

This is what successful people say, do, and when.

have said, "No, we can't". But can you see the double negative that just happened then too? "No, we can't" is a double negative, and we must avoid double negatives at all costs!

As an example, I will replace the negatives with the positives.

Q "Can you build a $10,000 website for only $8,000".

✗ "No, we can't" (That's how we feel. Maybe try...)

✓ "Yes, we can. We have some budget templates that may work for your budget instead".

✓ "I like how you think. Let's look at your options and if we can save you some money".

✓ "We would love to, although it's only $10,000 and is the best value you can get for what you need. It gives you all the attention to detail you asked for, and you want us to do your design properly, right"?

There are very few reasons why we need to say negative words. This includes our physical and written conversations. And the more positive and proactive we are in what we do, the more that has a mirror effect on what our leads hear.

So every time you write something in an email, look at your wording and replace all the negatives with positive language. Positive language is how people build their confidence and belief in our products and services. Because we're confident and optimistic with everything we say and do, and that's part of creating a positive environment for people to buy in.

Belittle the Price

One of the best things we can do is belittle our pricing on big-ticket items. Everyone loves a bargain or a good deal. So how do we do that? Well, a website is $10,000 or only $10,000.

Have you ever seen those infomercials repeating, "It's only"? That's because it works! And they constantly belittle their prices. So it's always

This is what successful people say, do, and when.

'only this' and 'only that' when pricing. Whatever that price is, "It's ONLY" is a perfect phrase to put at the front of all price conversations.

Pricing is always about value, and everyone loves a bargain. So when people hear the value is high and the price is low, there is more chance of a sale.

SYSTEM 13

The Cycle

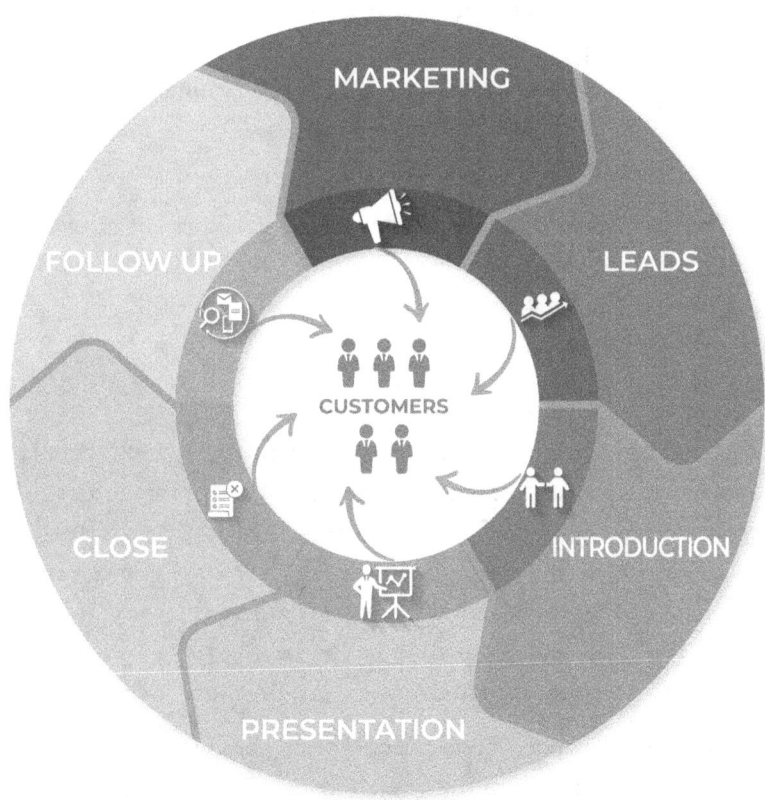

Let's have a look at my Business and Sales Cycle. This system is how most businesses and their sales systems work. And this is the exact system I followed to start and grow ReNet, and you can make this part of your systems too.

This is what successful people say, do, and when.

This system is excellent because we must know what to say, do, and when. Timing means saying the right things at the right times, and that's why the business and sales cycle works.

The Sides

The business and sales cycle works for every product or service we sell. Regardless of a large or small transaction, it's in every transaction as a fact. What's important here is also to know there are two sides. There's the side of us that understands and uses it to sell, and then there's the other side, the people experiencing and going through it as they buy. So it's a map of where people are as they engage or interact with us and our products and services. But it's our responsibility to understand and leverage it so we both achieve value.

System 1357®, the 1 is people first. The two sides mean we always look at what's in it for customers. We are going through it, and so are they.

Beginning and Ending

The good news is that there's also no specific entry point. People can start anywhere and anytime. Selling does not have a time limit, so there are no time limits in any of the Business and Sales Cycle stages either. Plus, there is no specific endpoint either. It's a cycle! People can start, go around and exit or buy at any stage, and then the cycle continues. However, the goal is to get people to the heart of the cycle, your hot zone. The more people are in your hot zone, the more success you have.

For example, if you are considering buying something and going into a store, you probably don't need their introduction, but their presentation is required regardless of their service. On the other hand, if you already wanted to buy something, you'd probably go straight to the close and look for the best price, service, or delivery options. All your signals are, "Can you tell me more about why I should buy and buy from you". Then the seller would (hopefully) go through their cycle and create the environment for you to buy in. Now think about how many times you have been around this cycle as a buyer, all the different stages you've entered, maybe when you purchased a car, smartphone, clothes, computer, holiday, etc. As buyers, we are all at different stages of buying readiness. So as a seller, it's your responsibility to work the cycle and constantly train for each stage in your systems for both them and us.

So recognising where people are in the cycle is critical. I mean that if someone you spoke to last year wanted to buy something from you today from a follow-up, that would be great, wouldn't it? So if someone will become your client today, next month, in six months, or even next year, that's still okay. You are winning as long as they don't take their money and spend it with your competition.

Overselling and Underselling

I bet you've gone into a shop at least once and wanted to buy, but you didn't get any service, so you didn't buy anything and left. So you think, "I will go somewhere else and spend my money with someone who wants it". Why? Because you were undersold, you weren't shown any love. We have all had that happen, haven't we?

And I bet you have been into a shop where you were oversold, you went in to buy one thing, now they're telling you about five different things, and you go, now I'm confused, so you decide to think about it instead. Why? Because we were oversold. We have all had that happen, too, haven't we?

Overselling and underselling are common, so it's essential to know and understand these systems to serve people correctly according to where they are in the cycle. And when done right, and we get the opportunity and seize it, we get more people into the centre of our business cycle. That means they have become clients and are now in our hot zone. And then, when we retain them as long-term clients, they generally want to buy more from us as we continue the evolution of our Business and Sales Cycle.

Generally, people are good at one-half of the cycle. For example, someone gets sales from the people they talk to but need more people to talk to to make more sales. So they are good at the introduction, presentation and close but need to work on their follow-up, marketing and lead generation. Alternatively, someone who talks to many people but isn't making many sales. They are great at marketing, leads and introduction but must work on their presentation, close and follow-up.

Everyone has a strong side and an improvement side. So the rest of these systems take you through how to improve what you are good at and how to make the most out of what you need to improve.

Make Your Own

Most people turn up to work, have a routine they go through and while doing that, respond to any people or enquiries that come in. But that's not really a system. That's simply responding. That's not really selling, is it?

Let me get specific now with what to say, do, and when, so you can make more sales and make more money! I will start the cycle from leads for no other reason than if I started a business from zero again, I would begin with generating leads. So it's a perfect starting place for the cycle.

Also, when I ask most people what their system is for sales, only a few can write it down as a flow chart or repeat what they say, do, and when. Can you? It's OK if you can't. Most can't. It's perfectly normal, so relax. This is why you are reading this. Even so, I want to challenge you. I want you to use what you know in addition to these systems and strengthen what you already use and understand. So… What are your steps? What do you say, do, and when? Is it duplicatable and trainable to other people? Can you explain it?

So let's create your system and use the workbook to do it.

This is what successful people say, do, and when.

SYSTEM 14

Introduction

Let's quickly think of a traditional Indian hunter from the old days. When they were hunting and saw some deer, do you think their first reaction was to jump up and down to make lots of noise? No, that would scare their dinner away, right? It would also be useless hiding behind the bushes waiting half asleep or just watching the deer eating the trap waiting to see what happened In the old days, hunters did not eat unless they caught a deer. So how they introduced themselves (or didn't) to deer while hunting once they saw them was the dictator of whether they ate dinner, or not.

Let me give a real-life example. So I wanted to buy my wife a new car. I had just had a deal fall through with a car I had ordered with Lexus. I was driving past my local Mercedes Benz dealer, and a car in the yard

This is what successful people say, do, and when.

caught my eye. It's the same dealer I purchased my first car from in 1990. I phoned and made an appointment to test drive at 12:30 Saturday. I'm there early, walk around and then go into the showroom right on time. There was no salesperson there. That's OK. I sat down and waited on the couch near the salesperson's desk. The salesperson eventually comes in with a husband and wife. He didn't acknowledge me. That's OK. He was busy. Minutes later, he got up to show them something outside. I waited again. When they returned, I'd made a cup of tea and remained on the lounge. At 1:00 pm, I was closed-minded, left and didn't drive or buy that car.

I didn't look like a Mercedes buyer in the salesperson's defence. I had just returned from 6 weeks travelling in Tasmania. Plus, the husband and wife were negotiating a new car each, and if it were me, I would be looking after the potential sale in front of me too. We can all understand and appreciate when someone is busy. The point here is that it was the way he made me feel. There was no quick introduction. I had an appointment with him, yet he ignored me. A brief introduction explaining what was happening would have worked. Acknowledgment and a smile would have been great too. Even worse, the dealer still hasn't phoned me to see why I didn't make the appointment. So I hope he sold the two cars to the couple, or else he lost three sales that day.

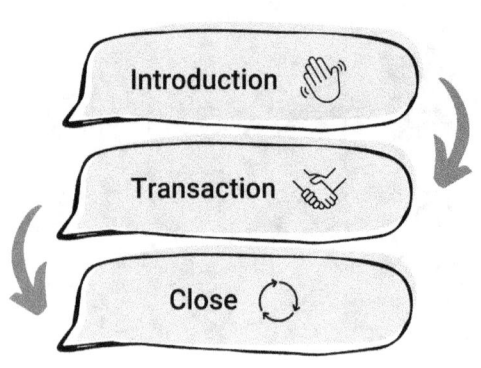

I know you are not like this car dealer. Even so, we can focus more on practising and perfecting our introductions. But why do we ignore perfecting our introductions? Because we always do introductions. So why bother practising them? Ask any athlete, and they will tell you that a good fast start is the key to winning the game. A positive introduction is the same for a cafe,

This is what successful people say, do, and when.

car dealer, retail shop, leader, and our success. And that's why we need to perfect it.

Introductions are your first action and reaction, setting up what happens next and, like an athlete, getting you a great start.

Remember, every interaction has 3 touch points, an introduction, transaction, and close. And even if you are speaking to someone for the 10th time, you still have your introduction touchpoint. That's why it's essential that you practice and perfect introductions.

4 Levels of the Human Mind

The rule of thumb at the introduction is that people are always open-minded. Thinking and being open-minded allows us to follow the system regardless of what the person asks. So we don't get fooled by false positives or negatives. We stay open and responsive.

There is no harm in open-minded thinking from both of us. But there is in us being overconfident. So a great introduction is designed to make everyone comfortable in our buying environment.

If we want people to open up and listen to us, we must be open-minded and listen to them. We must be excellent listeners using our two ears and one mouth. So the whole point of our introduction is to get into our presentation; the best way to give that is for them to ask for it. Then we can say, "I'm glad you asked", or "Let me show you". Then we can relax. And the more people ask questions, and we have the answers, we know we will get positive reactions from them because they have asked us for it.

This is not always that easy, and we know from the Business of Thirds® system that some people in our introduction want to try and close us off, some people will be easy to open up, and others will go either way depending on what we do. For example, when someone visits a car dealership, they didn't go there to buy flowers or shoes, did they? They have cars on their mind. There's an interest. And as salespeople, it's our job to introduce ourselves, open their minds, have a conversation, and then solve their problems or satisfy their needs.

We don't judge a book by its cover, and we don't judge a person by their lack of enthusiastic reaction to our introductions. As we open their minds, some people go deep into thought, so let them think. The good news is that they have come to talk and listen to us. So even if they are just open to asking questions or listening and seem not excited to buy right now, let them think, listen and ask us questions. With an open mind, people begin to build confidence and belief in your products and services, which is when they start to buy, and that only begins once you open their minds with your introductions.

Best Introduction Ever

Imagine if everyone we spoke to asked us to give them a presentation about our products. How much easier is that?

In 1990, I was taught this introduction just like you are now. I used it when selling insurance door-to-door. But I learned to master it and can't find a better one anywhere. So please write it down and memorise it. You can't fail when using this introduction. This works every single time. Yep, 100% of the time, even if you don't need to cold call for business.

When you say, "I believe THIS will interest YOU ALSO"! 100% of people think about two things. Firstly, show what's **THIS**? Then explain **WHO** also? And just like clockwork, they ask, "What is it"? "I am glad you asked", you reply. So not only have they asked what it is, but they have also asked you to show them what you are selling.

To extend this introduction, we can extend it by one or two words but keep it simple. It must stay succinct! For example, we used this at ReNet "I believe **this website** will interest **you also**". And when I was given a lead from Tom, I would say, "Tom believes **this** will interest **you also**". Can you see how these simple introductions perfectly open a lead's mind to have them ask, "What is it"? Even if they don't ask, they 100% think about it and want us to talk more about what we offer.

Let me break it apart and explain how to use it. Firstly, we don't say it in a monotone voice. The most critical parts to hear are **"this"** and **"you also"**. That's why I have highlighted them. We hesitate before and after, and we emphasise them. We do that because we want people to hear it and hear it really well. We need them to think or ask, "What is it" to permit us to talk more.

There is a reason why "I believe THIS will interest YOU ALSO" is on the book's cover. It works 100% of the time. Try it. Introduce it to your system too.

Inference

Ever seen a lineup for something and wondered what is so popular at the end of the line? For example, I've seen people line up for a cafe, making me believe it must be good if people are lining up for it.

And why do brands like Nike, Coke, and Red Bull sponsor people to wear their clothes and use their products? They need inference! Inference works. The good news is that we can use inference without costing us big sponsorship money. The inference is as easy as stating **"YOU ALSO"**. People like to buy what other people are buying.

One way I used inference in my introductions was a single name drop, then the **"you also"** introduction. Once again, when prospecting in the insurance days, I learned fast that whenever I went cold calling to use inference from a third person ASAP. I would do this by saying something like this "I was just talking to Tom. And we believe **this** will interest **you also!**". I would mention like-minded names because it added inference to my introduction. Most people wanted to know what I was talking to Tom about. And it worked every time.

Then after I say, "I believe **this** will interest **you also!**". I have to give the evidence to **you also**. There is no better way to build confidence and belief in our products and services than with people already using them to achieve their needs. Inference from others is perfect validation.

This is what successful people say, do, and when.

It would be silly to name-drop other people if I was selling coffee in a cafe, but we can still use inference. We can say things like, "What's been popular is". And if I am a Ford salesperson. I would say, "Tradies love these Ford trucks because they are unstoppable". The inference is simple to introduce and can be used in every introduction. Like at ReNet, it was "software ofter agents love".

In the instance business, we would show a list of names and businesses that were already insurance clients. Then, I'd briefly romance other clients and mention who they are. Something like "Tom from Tom's Mechanical" and "Mary with the Awesome Flowers on Main". Even if they didn't know Tom or Mary, they probably at least knew the business down the road.

Then at ReNet, we did the same thing. We'd show screenshots of existing agents' websites that we had built. Something like "Tom's Real Estate has a template site with five pages" or "Mary's Properties has a full custom site and a team of 50 spread out over five offices". Our slogan was "softer agents love".

Inference works but takes practice to perfect. So practice using the third person for inference in your introductions. It's a deliberate action used by all successful salespeople to win.

Begin With the End in Mind.

Have you ever seen an infomercial? They feel like 2-3 minutes of value, but wait, there's more. Then finally, in the end, they offer a special price. Of course, they always had a special price, but the value comes first. Price is at the end for a reason.

Buyers often begin at the end. They want a price so they can decide. Just like my wife, when she walks into a clothes shop, the first thing she does is look at the price tag. We all do that too. The difference for big-ticket items is that we keep pricing to the end unless you are just selling on price, such as when things are on sale/special. And in retail shops, it's done this way too. They display the price and let us decide. And

This is what successful people say, do, and when.

that's OK. They are small ticket items, and it would be silly to have a full presentation for pair of $150 jeans every time, wouldn't it?

I remember Tag Heuer Watches released a limited edition watch for a late Formula One driver. The reviewer said, "If you have to ask how much, you probably can't afford it". So the more exclusive, the less the price matters.

So what I mean by beginning with the end in mind is knowing that, as salespeople, we need to get buyers through our presentation before the end price. Once we talk about price, it's the end. Regardless of where we are in the cycle, pricing means you are now at your close.

Yes, we should always be closing. I am sure you have heard that before, and I will show you effective closes soon. But beginning with the end in mind means you don't jump to the end or close too soon. For example, we don't discuss pricing in our introductions. Pricing is always the last thing we speak about. So don't jump ahead. Stick to your system and cycle.

Buyers do the reverse, asking, "How much is it"? But that's because they are interested. Maybe starting to think, is this for me? They may seem all excited as they engage and ask questions, but we can't close yet. That's only once they are in a confident mind only. And that can only be after we've presented all our value to them.

So we start with something other than the price. During our introductions, they have yet to learn what's in it for them. So if we end too early, we could also be finished. We say a price, and they respond, "I am just looking" or "I'll just think about it". What do we do then? It's challenging to come back when someone says "no" during our introduction.

So once you know more about what they want on big-ticket items, you can give an accurate price on most products and services. They know that too. So beginning with the end in mind means we know where we want to go, and the close is in our minds, but we know that we have to go through the value proposition process and system first. Introduction, then presentation, and finally pricing and close.

This is what successful people say, do, and when.

What are some great comeback lines when someone asks, "How much is it"? In the intro, they are not really asking for the price. They're asking for more information. But we must answer their questions, don't we? Yes, we do! Some people are inclined to give some pricing examples, like "between $1,000 and $50,000 depending on what you want", which is an avoidance answer. Instead, try something like this "Let's get you the best price, firstly tell me more about…" or "It costs nothing to look at and very little to buy, so let me show you what's popular". That answers their question but not with the price. See how that's done?

Begin with the end in mind; you must get past your introduction and deliver your presentation. Why? If you don't, people will make a decision based on price. When you show them all their benefits and their value, there are more chances that leads will buy.

Your Objective

Our introductions are our first touchpoint whenever we get a lead or an inquiry. We respond with our introduction, which sets up the foundation of our sales system and opens people's minds as we take them through the 4 Levels of the Human Mind on our products and services. Introductions can be very quick and don't have to take long.

The secret is that our introduction must be constructive, and an introduction isn't all that fluffy stuff about how the weather is, what they did on the weekend, or what's on TV. So they are not effective introductions. It seems very nice that it's asked, but it's just a fluffy useless question with no real substance. That is unless you did want to know, but I bet you don't want to know how their weekend was, do you?

An effective introduction really is an introduction to us and our products and services. Depending on where we are in our cold, warm and hot zones matters next in our system. So what's the objective where we are now?

In a retail environment. I know they often ask, "Can I help you" to which we mostly reply, "No, I'm just looking". And that's still better

This is what successful people say, do, and when.

than ignoring people who walk into the shop. But the objective should be to engage with them on why they walked in and open their mind to the products in the shop.

I had a do-it-now face-to-face or Belly-to-Belly presentation objective when I was cold calling. If not, my objective was to schedule a time when I could control the buying environment, and we were both physically and mentally in a warm zone.

My objective at a networking event, bar, or BBQ is to schedule something next rather than start my presentation there. Get them to my shop, or I go to them or meet them somewhere for a coffee. Trying to sell someone outside of our zones is not going to work. So the intro objective is to meet them in our zones.

With an email, our objective is to respond quickly yet succinctly with something positive in reply and mention we will phone them, but then if the time is good for you, phone them straight away (I've won business this way). Your objective may be to schedule a better time, but you aim to keep a buyer warm with a warm initial introduction.

We are constantly doing introductions, but successful people know their objectives and follow the system, as timing is everything. So as you write down your system and process, think about the many situations you use your introductions and what you need to do to achieve your end objective. Knowing your objective means your stay in control of your environment.

Elevator Pitch

How often are we asked, "What do you do for a living"?

This can be at a BBQ, bar, networking event, on holidays, etc. This is when our elevator pitch and introduction work. People want to know in a few seconds what we do, and we should exude confidence and belief in ourselves. This sometimes is the very first introduction people get from us.

This is what successful people say, do, and when.

Get used to doing your elevator pitches, practising them, and confidently saying them. Saying what you do and what you have to offer. 20 or 30 seconds is your introduction. At ReNet, I would say things like, "I specialise in business websites that help people grow their businesses in the real estate industry". Now it's "I am a self-funded retiree, and I now share street smart systems with people worldwide so they can work smarter, not harder".

Use keywords, and say what value you bring and what's in it for them within seconds.

On the receiving end is someone who's thinking, "Who is this person", "What do they do" and "Is there anything for me". The good news is that if there is, you can get their number and schedule something, and if there is no interest, they at least know what you do.

People want to know what your specialty is. So an effective elevator pitch is one of your introductions.

Retail Examples.

Salesperson: "Can I help you"?

Buyer: "I am just looking"!

Salesperson: "Let me know if you have any questions"?

Often I hear a retail salesperson say that it's as though they thought, "Phew", so now they can go back to standing behind the counter. But, as you can see, the "Can I help you" introduction breaks all the rules.

Now, this is not the store salesperson that's at fault. They often are not trained in sales. As a result, they do not know what to say, do, and when. So they walk up and try but ask close-minded questions. And now you know why "Can I help you" breaks all the rules.

It's easy for us to see who the store owners are by their introduction or if the business does regular training to develop their staff great introductions.

And there's a better way of asking, "Can I help you" like these.

This is what successful people say, do, and when.

Salesperson: "We have new season stock that I believe will interest you also. They are very popular! Let me show you over here".

Salesperson: "Hello, some of the newest ABCs have been popular. Let me show you.

You want your introductions to set you up for your constructive presentations and increase your strike rate. So it's more than "How are you going"? "Can I help you"? "How's the weather"?

Successful salespeople deliberately and intentionally start with a practised and trained introduction. So Write down and create your introductions, and make your best introductions ever. Then like a professional athlete, practice them. Practice! Practice! Practice! Record yourself if you have to, but get unreal at opening people's minds with your rock-solid introductions.

SYSTEM 15

Presentation

"Hey mum, where do babies come from," my son asked his mum. "Go ask your father", she said. My son said, "It's ok. I don't want to know that much about it". HAHAHAHA

OK, so my son didn't actually ask that, but we always joked about this situation in sales training. Because some people haven't been trained in how to sell. Your sales presentation is as simple as an open two-way interactive conversation with intent rather than your sales pitch. You can even remove the word sales entirely and replace it with conversation.

Because this is now when you and your clients do the most talking, Your presentation is where you will see the most fluctuation in the 4 Levels of the Human Mind. But this is also when you do have some control. You are the driver of the reactions you get from our actions, what you say, do, and when. So your presentation must be structured to build confidence in you and your products before you close or talk about money and seal the deal. And I would have loved it if I'd gotten a sale every time I spoke to a buyer, but that's not how it works!

The good news is that increasing your strike with your presentations is easy. I have already introduced many systems to you earlier in this book and explained how effective these systems are and how they make your structured conversations work for you. So read them again.

Meantime, I'll bring it together for you. You're going to love these in addition to what you have already learnt.

Stop Selling

The presentation is where all the magic happens as you begin discussing your products and services. You've qualified the buyer, and you've delivered your introduction. Now, with permission, they want to know more about your products and services. So now you go to work.

But stop selling!

The secret here is that even though this is your turn to talk and you are presenting, you are having a conversation rather than doing a presentation. You're taking people on a journey through the 4 Levels of the Human Mind, and your presentation or conversation is the best time to bring people from open to confident or belief and get your yes answer. So, yes, I know you'll do a lot of the talking, but remember to stop selling. The objective of your presentation is to find out where their hot spot, pain, or needs are, and depending on the price of what we sell, this may be seconds, minutes, hours, days, weeks or months.

Remember, people buy two things, they buy us, and they buy your products and services. And they have to be confident in both, or else we'll miss a sale. For example, we might want a Ford, but when we walk into their dealership and don't like the service or salesperson, we're going to go to another Ford dealer and spend our money, aren't we? So it's not the product that was the issue. The salesperson or business did not understand their sales systems. So, yes, you need to have excellent product knowledge and be able to present it but also in an understanding conversational manner that gets results.

Sales conversations are very intentional and with purpose. After all, they didn't come to us to make friends. Instead, they are interested in something we have. The good news is that making your conversations work is as easy as all systems I wrote about earlier in the book. FAB conversations, conversations in your cold, warm and hot zones, reading their body language, the power of great questions, and involving clients.

As you discuss your products and services, your conversations will take people on a journey of the 4 Levels of the Human Mind. In reply, they are testing you as they listen. They are testing if they will spend their money with you. And if your conversation passes their tests, you should get a yes, or better still, someone buying your products and services without having to sell. So stop selling and think of it as a conversation.

3 Reasons

This is what makes us buy? It's because we have a problem or we want something, true?

So what is the buyer's problem? Or what do they want? The good news is that knowing the problem or buying motivation is optional. They can tell us what they are, but we don't need to find them, and we don't go asking about them either. They will tell us if they want. But all we need to know to do is fulfil one of the 3 motivations behind every transaction: hot spot, pain, or a need (HPN). Let me quickly explain.

1. Hot Spots are when someone is motivated to buy something. It's only a want. There are no problems or pain, it's not urgent, and it's not needed or essential. It's a desire, a reward, and not a necessity. For example, I don't need a new car, but I like the look of the latest release. Or next summer, a new Jetski or a bigger deck on the house for entertaining would be great. New clothes are classic; we buy them because they make us feel good, not because we don't have any clothes already, but because we want something new. We don't actually need them. We want them.

2. Pain Point. There is something wrong, and the pain makes it essential to find a solution. My car has broken down and is unrepairable, so I must get another one to get to work. It's now, and it's urgent! When someone is in pain, then sales are more straightforward. Nobody negotiates with the plumbers weekend rates when a pipe bursts on the weekend, do they? Nobody negotiates with the mechanic when they have a breakdown and need it fixed ASAP, do they? When we need to get a flight at the last minute, and it's super expensive, no problem, we'll pay. It's the pain from not having something that out ways the cost. If the pain from the problems is big enough, we will pay whatever it takes, won't we? So selling to someone's pain is the easiest.

Needs, this is somewhere in between our motivational hot spot and the pain point. I need it, but it's not urgent and not causing any problems. For example, my car is getting old, and I'll need a new one eventually. Again, there's no pain (yet), and it's not motivating me just now, either, but I know I will need one. So I'll start to go to dealerships and look around and research. But again, it's not urgent or important (yet).

The good news is that as salespeople, we can either fulfil and need or create a need. So if someone has a need for your products and services, you can meet their needs. Or you can develop needs by analysing what people would like to buy and then create a need. So, in other words, the good news is that you can actually create needs people didn't think they had.

As buyers, when we need something, we often start to research what we want to buy and what the best buys are, don't we? Like walking into a car dealership to see if something sparks our interest.

So Solve It!

The 3 reasons people put their hands in their pockets are hot spots, pain, and needs. So solve these for them, and if they're satisfied, they'll spend whatever it takes.

Hot spots and pain are easier to sell because those buyers are more motivated to do it now. On the other hand, needs require you to use more of your systems to increase your strike rates. When something is not a burning desire to buy for someone or solve their immediate problems, you need to do more work if you want them to spend their money with you instead of with your competition (or elsewhere).

How do we find their motivation?

As you go through your presentation and conversation, generally, people will begin to reveal what motivated them to talk to us. And as they get more comfortable with you and grow to know, like, and trust

This is what successful people say, do, and when.

you, they will tell you more. Sometimes it's very upfront. For example, "My car has broken down", "my plumbing is leaking", or "I love the latest model car". And their questions reveal their true motivation too. For example, the "how much as I need it now" shows their true motivation, a pain point! But most people take a little nurturing before they trust you with their why.

Do you need to know what is motivating them to buy? No! It's great to know, but it doesn't matter. Some people only tell us after they buy what the real reason was that they purchased from us. So, in other words, it does not matter. It's only essential that if they want what you have, they spend their money with you and not your competition, true?

You don't go to the Ford dealer when you're thinking about flowers, do you? But there is a reason why you did. And the same for your potential clients. They have a reason they want to talk to you, and even though you don't need to know the reason, it's there if you listen for it.

3 Reactions

Eventually, we all decide yes or no as buyers. Of course, the bigger the sale price, the longer our decision may take, but even with a $5 coffee, it's still a yes or no reaction. Now many people think there are only 2 buyer reactions, yes or no! But there is also "I'll think about it". Which is "I'm interested but have not seen a reason to buy yet".

Obviously, the reaction you want to avoid is a "no". That's why high-achieving salespeople have multiple reasons, allowing someone to say "yes" and leaving very few reasons for a "no". When they are in conversation with a lead, they keep that lead in the palm of their hands and in control of their buying environment. Your goal is a "yes", and the buyer's goal is a great buy or solving their problems.

When we use the Business of Thirds® system, a third of people will say "yes", a third will say "no", and a third can go either way, depending on what we say, do, and when. In the next chapter, I talk about your close, and that's when it's time to get your answer. First, however, you need a systematic approach to increase your strike rate and move more

This is what successful people say, do, and when.

buyers to your top and positive third whenever you give your presentation.

The better you are at all of these systems, the more you will achieve the two outcomes you want, whether a sale now or a deal in the future. So a yes decision now is excellent, but don't get annoyed if someone says they want to think about it and leaves. That happens to the best of us. If you get upset, they may never come back. One of the easiest sales you'll ever make is when someone comes back to buy in the future when you spoke to them some time ago.

The bottom line is that if someone wants your products or services, then why not yours? And if someone wants to buy from us now or later, that's OK too. So do whatever it takes to avoid the no, try to achieve a yes, but keep them in the buying mood for when they are ready to buy.

Buyers are Liars!

"Sorry, Scotty, I don't have the time right now". But 2 hours later, I walked out with a cheque.

"Sorry, Scotty, I don't have any money to spend right now". But 2 hours later, I walked out with a cheque.

Ok, it's not that they were lying. It's that they were not being honest with me. So I learned to ignore their initial reasons not to listen to me. I do the same. And whenever you're buying big ticket items, you don't always lay all your cards on the table either, do you? No! Of course not! Because we're all a little protective of our motivation or real reasons we're buying. We don't always reveal our hot spot, pain, or need. So buyers are liars to be protective. Learn to respect that, knowing it's perfectly OK for them to hold on to their cards, too, just like we do.

For example, when I was a sales rep in the 90s, I learnt to avoid driving into a motel to negotiate better prices for a week's stay. I would walk in. That meant they didn't judge me by my car. And I generally got a better deal! The funny thing is, I now have old run-about cars, so whenever I go anywhere to buy, I dress down and take the old cars, never the good ones. Why? I didn't want people to add a luxury tax because they thought I could afford to pay more. Although, sometimes, that also meant I didn't get served, another mistake by the salesperson.

I know many people are weak and can only sell on price. So when I would ask if this was their best price, and I looked like I couldn't afford it, it's incredible how often they'd give me a great deal to get a sale.

Another example, I once met Peter Grey. He built a ten-story house in the country between Booral and Buladelah in NSW, Australia. (Thought to be the tallest residential building in the southern hemisphere) To no surprise, he also drove luxury cars. The story goes that he would wear his old dairy farm clothes when he bought new vehicles. He didn't look like he could afford the cars he was looking at. Legend has it that one time when he was buying, the salesman didn't serve or ignored him. So Peter went to the manager and said he would buy it if he sacked the salesman. I don't know if it's true, but I met Peter, and he was just like us, a regular guy who had created tremendous wealth. He just wanted to be himself when he was buying. Oh, and Peter didn't buy any insurance from me! I did try twice, though, LOL...

Another common event in real estate was that someone would look at a three-bedroom property in a specific location and tell the agent that that's all they could afford. Many agents would believe them. Only to see a few months later that the buyer had purchased a house in a different suburb with four bedrooms and spent more money. Because the buyer either didn't want to share their actual buying ability or they found something they wanted and stretched their buying ability to match. I spent almost 20 years teaching real estate agents how to sell, and new people in the industry believed the buyers. But the buyers can often buy more and will buy differently if the right property comes along. So it's not that they lied, but the truth was different.

So what's different with your presentations? Nothing! Buyers are liars because your clients are being protective of themselves, and it's perfectly natural for them to do so. But it's up to us to read between the lines and find one of the 3 reasons they will buy because of their HPN.

So never judge a book by its cover.

The Competition

The worst outcome we can get in sales is when someone buys what you have but spends their money with your competition. That hurts more than a "no" answer.

Let me repeat that when someone talks about your competition to you, **that's good news!** Because they still haven't purchased yet, and they haven't with your competition either, have they? But they are now talking to you, so **this is your opportunity to be a better salesperson and** make a sale.

Over the years, I have had many people talk about me as their competition when selling. Whilst I don't argue, I do wonder why? For me, who is the competition anyway? I am better than them. Over time I'll learn about them anyway. But who cares? I focus on what I have as I don't get paid for selling their stuff, do I? And to be honest, I never do any research on the competition, which may surprise you, but why would I? I don't sell their products. I will never talk about them. So why would I waste time researching them? I did get to know who there were, but I ignored them and only focused on my buyers.

Nonetheless, it's important to your buyers sometimes. So what do we do when someone talks about your competition? They say, "That company does this", or "does that", or, "I think theirs is good because". So how do you handle these situations?

Firstly, what the competition does is unimportant, regardless of whether a comment is positive or negative. What you do is we Business Judo® them and deflect over into what you offer. They want to know what's your value proposition. What are your advantages and benefits? They haven't bought it yet, but they want to buy. They're building their confidence and know, like and trust in you. Again, you can't sell other people's products and services, but you can sell the products and services you have. And that's why they are talking to you, and they still have a reason to buy that is not fulfilled.

When people talk about your competition in your presentations, they reveal their hot spot, pain, need, and motivation. So them talking about your competition is good news. So it's now your turn to shine as your competition hasn't!

You're Being Tested

I used to love walking into a restaurant and not reading the menu. I would ask the person serving me, "What's good on the menu" and watch their reaction. I wanted them to sell me the best meal they had. Some people got it, but many didn't. Some people would say, "If you want a steak, we have some great special, or there's fresh locally caught fish", as they'd go in romancing the menu. Yet others had no idea! Some even said, "I haven't eaten here". Seriously, they are in the front of this shop, telling me they don't even know what the food is like.

The thing is, most buyers want to be sold to. I know that sounds the reverse of what I have been talking about, but let me explain.

I am saying that as buyers, we want the person serving us to do their job, don't we? We want to know why we should buy. And the way we do that is to test them. We'll ask questions and wait for their answers. And your buyers are the same. Most people want to test you, ensure you know what you're talking about, and build up know, like, and trust.

Sometimes they already know the answer too. But they want to see if we agree with them, have a better idea, or even that we're being honest and truthful. That's why we need to be very honest with buyers, they might be liars, but we never are!

Testing us is an excellent thing. When they're questioning you in your presentation, it means they want to buy from you. In other words, what they ask with their questions is, "Tell me why I should buy from you"?

One Feature at a Time

The best way to give a feature-rich presentation is by speaking about one feature at a time. But, unfortunately, it's common for new salespeople to oversell and start talking about ALL the different features without FABing the one that a buyer has asked about, as that's the feature that's their HPN. In other words, they complicate things and create reactions that drive buyers away from a yes to a maybe.

When someone wants your product or service for one reason, that's the only reason you need. However, it is incredible how often we hear people presenting and they oversell, talking about things they have yet to be asked about.

So keep things nice and simple. One feature at a time. For example, at ReNet, we had five streams of income or products. So if needed, I'd mention the five, and then they would ask about one of them, say the CRM, so that's their HPN, and then that's all we needed to sell to satisfy them. So we made sure they bought the CRM and fulfilled their HPN.

So focus on HPN and nail that one. And when we had a client say "yes" and buy that, the job was done, and everyone is happy! We can always use the upsell later, or they can always come back and buy more, too, can't they? They may not need those other features, and we didn't confuse leads with things they aren't interested in either. So keep selling simple.

For example, if I was in a mechanic shop that also sold tyres. When someone comes in to get their car serviced, I will service it first. And then I might mention, did you want some new tyres, or when they come in for the tyres, I solve that problem first, then I might say, by the way, would you like to get your car serviced too? But if when they came in, and I tried to sell both tyres and service, that would now be overselling because a simple HPN transition has become complicated.

Present one feature, or solve one problem at a time. Of course, you can always package more up later, but if you initially oversell in your presentation, leads can become confused, and you end up with nothing.

Emails are NOT Your Presentation

Emails, websites, and brochures do not sell, and they are NOT your presentation either. If you think they are your presentation, then you're using a send and hope as part of your sales system. There's a better way. Let me explain.

A brochure in an email may work great for the $19.90 pizza deals. But if you are in sales, your email, brochure, or website **does not** replace you. You can use them but know that they will not do your job for you, or else we wouldn't need you to sell, would we? You do the selling, not your email, brochure, or website.

For example, when I was selling ReNet, maybe a website design. I would get people to go to our website, and I'd walk through the website design examples with them. But see what I was doing? I didn't email them telling them to go to the website, look at it and then get back to me. I didn't leave them and expect our website to do the selling for me, and it didn't do a close for me either. But I used our website as a presentation prop, not as a replacement salesperson.

A written email isn't a prop either. Many rookie salespeople send awesome emails full of excellent information and pricing, finished with "let me know if you have any questions", and then expect a "yes" reply. When buyers don't, the salesperson then wonders why people are not buying after such an excellent email. It's because; an email is not a salesperson. Even though a salesperson writes it, they mistakingly think that their email is as amazing as them, but it's not!

Many people get email leads asking for more information. But they'll reply and put an excellent sales presentation and pricing into their email response. It's an attempt to answer all their questions, and often it's even a copy-paste reply with a brochure attached. After all, it's what the lead asked for. So if you do this, don't!

The worst system I have seen is when someone attaches a contract to their email. Like that will excite a buyer, a black-and-white contract with all their price and terms and conditions. I'd be so excited to receive that, wouldn't you? But instead, the body language of the email is saying; here's the price and our contract if you want it. What does that system do with the 4 Levels of the Human Mind? A contract may work with someone at the belief level, but for everyone else? It's a mind closer! This is why people say, "I've sent lots of quotes out, but my strike rate is terrible".

So what do you do? How do you send emails and get a result?

When you're selling a higher ticket item, then this is where working your sales system works. Knowing your email's objective, as in your email is not to sell. It's only correspondence and general information and should be used only to get a buyer to the next proper presentation, belly-to-belly.

Your email should be written so that it gets buyers to ask for more information or expect us to show more as part of their buying cycle. This is how your emails are used to create your buying environment. And your buying environment works best when it's face to face, on a video call, or picking up the phone, and not on your email, brochure, or website. Nothing replaces you as a salesperson.

How Much Is It?

You're in the middle of your conversation, and your buyer asks, "How much is it"? What a great sign. It's possibly a sign that your buyer is moving up in the 4 Levels of the Human Mind. Maybe they are gaining confidence in us and our products. But it's often the same answer as always. They are asking, "I'm interested, but can I have more information before I buy".

But how do you know the difference between someone asking for pricing so they can say "yes" or "no' and someone asking because they have gained confidence and are possibly ready to buy? Here's an example, where does this lead seem to be? "How much is it for the red one"? They are starting to indicate a preference, showing that what you have been doing so far is working. They're starting to talk about ownership of your product by talking about their colour preference as they buy from your presentation and environment, aren't they? So your answer would be something like a test close, "The red one is great. Is that your preference"? Their response will confirm their thinking for you.

The point here is that the price question could be their way of being able to say "no". Or their way to get you to the point so they can say "yes". Remember, potential buyers are always trying to test you, and if they're losing interest, sometimes they'll ask, "How much is it" so they can say, "I'm not interested. I can't afford it. Or I will think about it".

If you go straight into pricing with the answer, "It's $4,000", or depending on your pricing, which could be $40,000 or $400,000", guess what? You've now gone into pricing, meaning you are now closing the sale. Or you are now selling on price and not the value. So talking price means you have progressed past your presentation and onto closing, which is why knowing your sales system is critical, as you'll know what we will say, do, and when.

What I am saying is that the last thing you talk about is price, it's the first thing they want to know, but once you are talking about your prices, it's much harder to go back to the presentation. So the bigger the price, the more it's the last thing you talk about because the price is in your close.

Quiz

While writing this book, I did a test on a DM from LinkedIn.

How many mistakes can you find? Can you find at least 10?

There are over 20 rookie sales mistakes. (Ignore grammar)

 Haseeb Haider · 10:52 PM
Hi Scotty,

I hope you are doing well!

I know this sounds out of nowhere but I wanted to reach out and see if you are looking for a freelance assistant.

As a freelancer, I mainly provide the services of:

1) LinkedIn outreach and organic marketing
2) Front-end web development

Are you interested in it? If not, can you please direct me to your colleague who will find my services useful?

I hope I'm not overstepping with this reach-out, but if you think I did, I apologize in advance. I know you absolutely get several of these a day but I've learned if you don't ask, the answer is always no.

Thanks,
Haseeb Haider

PS: since I'm a freelancer/independent contractor, my charges are very competitive as compared to marketing agencies.

 FRIDAY

 Scotty Schindler · 6:15 AM
How much?

 Haseeb Haider · 8:52 PM
It depends but to give you a range, the base pricing of LinkedIn services starts from $300 - $700 USD

What is your primary usage of LinkedIn? I see you have a good number of followers and also you are posting every day which is super important!

You are not using any hashtags I'm not sure why but if you don't wanna use the conventional/trending hashtags at least you should come up with your own hashtag. You are posting content on a daily basis so you can easily dominate and make a branded hashtag for yourself.

What do you think?

Quiz answers are on the book's webpage at www.system1357.com

SYSTEM 16

Close

Did you know a crocodile has almost a 100% stake rate when it attacks its pre? A crocodile will sit and wait for the perfect time to strike an unsuspecting animal on the river bank. It is patient and will lay hidden in the water unseen, but when the time is right, and they know its efforts will be successful, it will attack, but **only** when it believes it will succeed. They know that if they go too early, they will scare away their feed. So timing is everything.

And your close is the same, and you should only use it when the time is right. Your close is after the presentation or when you believe someone is more likely to say "yes", and that's when they are confident to buy, or they are asking buying questions, and you can't close a sale before that. It isn't easy to return to your introduction or presentation once you start to close.

It's said to "Always Be Closing" (ABC), and that's true. But I will show you how and not to scare away buyers. Just like a crocodile, you don't want to scare away your feed by making false attempts and closing too early.

I know you want an excellent strike rate. And you are doing the work anyway, so why not make it easier on yourself? So let me change how you think about closing altogether. You will love this. Now is when you get paid!

Your 3 Closes

Unlike the crocodile, we can understand what our leads are thinking first. That's because we have 3 closes we can use. Yep, 3!

Your 3 closes are 1. Test, 2. Soft, and 3. Hard

We know that at some point, we must ask our closing question. And I believe that if you're good at your conversations, you should never have to give a hard close. I mean that people should buy from you before you even need to use your hard close, but sometimes you do need to get a final answer, and that's when you use your hard close.

Many people do not know that the 3 closes even exist, let alone how to use them. If you can't write yours down, then you don't have them, so you're normal. But when it's time to ask buyers for their business so you get paid, you can use any of the 3.

Firstly, my preference is that you should never need to give a hard close. Some sales coaches will tell you that you've got to do hard closes, but I will show you how to use all 3. Let me explain them quickly.

Your test close is ultra subtle, even suggestive, and you use open words like 'prefer'.

Your soft close is warm, using directional words such as 'like'.

Your hard close is final, using closing words such as 'want'.

Most people I coach have never thought of these 3, especially the test close, but expert salespeople continuously test close through their conversation. Why? Because test closes tell you where the buyer is on the 4 Levels of the Human Mind. Are they closed, open, confident, or believe? If they are not confident yet in us or our product, and we use a hard close and get a "no", it's much harder to keep the conversation going. So a test close is what you use to keep the conversation open.

For example, back to the Ford dealer, let's say they were talking to a buyer and looking at a blue car. They could say, "The Ford comes in a range of colours, this blue, red, silver, or black. What colours do you prefer"? Did you see how Socrates Successful Method was used first, followed by a test close? It also fits with the power of great questions too. Regardless of their answer, the car salesperson will have somewhere to go next. If a buyer responds negatively with, "I don't like any of the colours", what does that tell them? They are a bit closed-minded, aren't they? But they can then ask, "What other colours do you prefer"? So this test close again has allowed them to get more information. And if they say, "I like red cars" or "Can I get a metallic colour"? What are they doing? Buying! They have just said yes to our test close. Yet all we've asked is a nice suggestive like and preference question.

And the soft close is firmer, "What colours do you like"?

And the hard close if final "What colours do you want"?

See the difference.

Test = "What colours do you prefer"?

Soft = "What colours do you like"?

Hard = "What colours do you want"?

At ReNet, we said things like this;

Test = "What websites do you prefer"?

Soft = "What websites do you like"?

Hard = "What websites do you want"?

These are elementary examples. But think of all the test, soft, and hard closes you have or use.

Your test closes are used constantly during your presentations. And when you get good at your test closes, they become the most used close you use because people start saying "yes" to you sooner. In addition, test closes allow you to pick up on their buying signals and respond as needed.

Hard closes, hopefully, you never need to ask a hard-hitting closing question, but sometimes we do. Sometimes we need to know if this is worth pursuing or not. I prefer that you get good at delivering your test

This is what successful people say, do, and when.

closes and ask them as often as possible, so you don't need a hard close. But then again, if you have to give a hard close, by all means, deliver your hard close.

Sometimes must ask a closing question. So when I had been selling to someone for a while at ReNet, a few emails and phone calls later etc. It's then time to use a final close, like, "Tom, we can complete your new website in around two weeks. It's only a 50% deposit, so let's do it. So only $5,000 today. Let's lock you in for your new website. Is that OK"?

I will definitely get their answer from something like that close, won't I? I used this only when I believed that Tom was confident in the company, myself and the product. Or if I feel we are not getting anywhere and need a final answer.

As another example, recently, I had to use a hard close for a coaching client. They had reached out a few times for coffee and catch-ups. And I am OK with that as that's prospecting with someone in my warm zone. But one day, it was time. "Scotty, can we catch up"? I said, "Yes, happy to catch up, but let's formalise this! Let's put a proper development program in place, so you know you are getting the best of me. OK"? They replied, "I'll let you know". In other words, the free sessions were over, and it was time they paid, so I had to hard close them, but only when the time was right. We still don't have a deal at the time of writing, but I am OK with that. Because that's why I used a hard close, it was time, and I needed to know where we were.

The close we used in the insurance industry was a series of hard closing questions straight after we used inference from existing clients, which worked great! Remember, we were always face-to-face as this was door-to-door selling. Our body language was so important at the close; we would look at our folders and make eye contact at different times. When we closed, we'd turn our folder and make eye contact, put our pen on an empty insurance contract, and positively nod our head and say… "all we need is your name and address. For example, (looking down at our examples) here's Peter, Pam and Bill". Then we'd turn and look at our lead with direct eye contact, put our pen in the writing position, and continue with, "So, if you don't mind? I would like to write one for you also! If you don't mind? May I do that for you? May I"? (We then shut up, nod our head subtly and positively, and wait with eye contact). When done right, this worked! We got our answers, signed them up, or went to our rebuttals.

Test Closes = Can be asked anytime. You don't even need an answer for them. They may be rhetorical but are always open questions to which you believe they will respond positively.

Soft Closes = Similar to a test close, but you should get an answer. Again, you are looking for directional and positive responses before you give your hard close.

Hard Closes = These are direct and get you a direct yes or no reaction. You have said as much as possible. So now it's time. You need to know where you stand. Are we doing a deal or not? Do you leave them alone and continue to work with other buyers?

The good news is that people can buy with any of your 3 closes. It's ok for people to say yes and any time. And you don't have to give a hard close to make a sale. I suggest you make your list of what you can use for your test, soft and hard closes.

Was That a Yes Answer

What's a yes answer anyway? Well, it doesn't need to be the word "yes". Trust me!

I know you think this is obvious, and it is, but I have seen this first-hand too many times. A buyer is saying yes, but in their own words, and the salesperson doesn't hear the "Yes" answer. "Yes" answers can be disguised as questions, for example.

"Can I get a big red one"?

"Can I get one today"?

"Can I get two"?

"How long will it take"?

This is what successful people say, do, and when.

"How much is the deposit"?

"What do I need to supply"?

"What are the extras I can get"?

Can you see how these are all yes answers? Now depending on what you have already asked, your reaction here will make a massive difference to your strike rates. You don't need to hear the word "YES". All you need is something like an "I want question".

The good news is that sometimes you don't even need to ask closing questions. Some people are ready to buy and give you an alternative "yes". But I see many salespeople keep selling after someone has said "yes" and then oversold and lose their sales altogether. People like buying and quickly buy because you created an excellent buying environment. When you are good at your presentations and using your test closes, you get yes answers long before you reach the end of your presentation. Then all you need to do then is thank them.

For example, when someone asks, "Can I have it delivered" we can say, "Yes, we've got them in stock, ready to go, and I'll get it for you". This deal is done as that was a yes answer.

"Scotty, can we get a new website finished by the start of next month"? "Yes, you can. Let's get you locked in". Can you see what has happened? We said "yes" to them, not them saying yes to us.

The good news is that people will say "yes" in many different ways. So, it's a great habit to ask them a test close to ensure you're reading the situation right. And when they ask, "Can I have it tomorrow" reply with something to close them, like, "Yes, I can get that organised. Does that work for you"? This way, we ensure it's not a false positive and was a "Yes, I'll buy".

Shut Up!

There is an old sales quote, "he who speaks first, loses".

So the secret to closing is to shut up! Say nothing and listen! It's your close, and you need a response! We need to give people the opportunity to buy. That's the point of your closes. So if you do a close and keep doing a presentation or keep talking, you may be overselling. So what you must do from time to time is stop and listen. And your closes are when you do that. You have asked a question, so it's their turn to talk.

OK, let me clear something up. Shut up, and listening is different to ignoring people. Shutting up and listening means allowing them to engage and reply to your conversations. Ignoring people or hoping they return after an email is a different kind of quiet. I refer here to our belly-to-belly conversations only.

Often when I was teaching people sales, I would see them do their test close, the buyer would want to answer and engage, but the salesperson would continue with their presentation. So if you ask a closing question but keep talking, you've just wasted an opportunity to obtain more information. Because their answer tells you what to say and do next. Generally speaking, when you use your close, it's because you've presented what you thought they were interested in, their hot spot, pain, or need. So now it's their turn to ask. Remember, you don't sell. People buy. Your closing is what lets them buy. And people love it.

I know that sounds so simple. And it is… Try it.

Close, stop talking, and listen.

Why Hard Close

For many people, closing a sale and asking the buying question is the scariest part because it's the physical act of asking people for their money. They get sweaty or cold feet about money, and they don't want to seem pushy. If this is you, then why hard close anyway? Let me explain.

Successful salespeople have an open introduction and an excellent presentation, so they rarely use a hard close. So the good news is that

This is what successful people say, do, and when.

often you don't need a hard close either. Many leads say "yes" to a well-structured presentation without you needing your hard close.

But your closes are for a reason, and if your test and soft closes have not received a "yes", then it does get to a point at the end of your presentation where you need to find out if they will say "yes" or "no".

My point is that when you've been presenting, the easiest way to get a "yes" answer early is by perfecting your test and soft closes and then listening for a yes reply. And leads appreciate you not being pushy because you're not slapping them with closes.

Lock the Sale Away

The buyer just said, "Yes". So what you do next matters, and it positively impacts the transition from buyer to a client. This one system alone sets apart successful salespeople from others. Let me explain.

Someone has just decided to buy from you. They have been wondering if they should spend their money with you. Now, they say, "Yes". So what's the first thing you say in reply to their "yes"?

Thank you! You finish the close with your appreciation.

For big-ticket items, we can do it a lot better than a quick "thank you". While that's a great start, someone has just committed to buying, they have gone from uncertain to sure, open to confident, buyer to a client, and we need to acknowledge them for their excellent decisions. After all, it was an excellent decision. They have chosen to give you their money, not give it to someone else. And that's excellent! True?

For example, at ReNet, "Tom, let's get started on your website"? "Ok, Scotty, send me an invoice". That's a yes, so what do I do now? If I am face-to-face, I handshake, and with eye contact, I say, "Congratulations, Tom, an excellent choice, and it's great to have you as a client. Thank you". If it's by phone or by email, I write it too. I always take the time to congratulate them and thank them for their business as they transition from buyer to client.

This is what successful people say, do, and when.

Tom has just decided to spend, say, $5,000, and he chose to spend it with me. And that's worth congratulating him on. True?

So their "yes" answer is your opportunity to lock the sale away and begin the client satisfaction journey. And this works in every single sale regardless of the cost, coffee, cars, or houses. Every time someone says "yes", congratulate and thank them for their decision. They have made an excellent decision, and they will be happy. It was brilliant, and they did it for all the right reasons. And it makes a massive difference when you acknowledge them and take them through the transition to the other side. This is a clear transition period and must be recognised in your sales systems. It's like watering plants you just purchased.

Back to the car salesperson, someone just said, "I'll buy a red one". The salesperson says (maybe shaking hands too), "Mr and Mrs Jones, great decision, the red car is perfect, you'll love it! Well done! Let's go do the paperwork". The buyers are acknowledged. They know they are no longer being sold. They are now a client, smiling and very happy. They're phoning Mum, Dad, and friends and posting on social media. And it's exciting to be a part of it as a salesperson.

Some people even have gift packs for new clients, but some miss the point. It's not a gift pack. It's an opportunity to do the client transition. Get eye contact and genuinely thank them for spending their money with you, not someone else. A gift pack is a great idea, but it has the most impact when done with genuine intention, and a thank you, and clients will appreciate you for what you do.

Think about it, their buying decision may have taken five minutes, hours, days, or months. Whatever, but they've now made a great decision to buy from you, that's why it's the first thing you do, recognise the excellent decision they have just made. When you do this, you see their whole attitude and emotions change. They are feeling good now because they have made a great decision. So put the icing on the cake and tell them how much you appreciate their business.

This is what successful people say, do, and when.

What is Overselling

This sounds impossible. But it happens all the time. For example, a salesperson gets a "yes" answer, and someone asks to buy, but the seller keeps selling. And when that happens, it confuses the buyer and results in a negative response, generally a "no" answer. So the buyer leaves and tries someone else who understands them, like your competition.

I have seen salespeople get a "yes"; then, five minutes later, they get an "I'll think about it" response. "I thought I had a sale," they say. "Well, they did, but you didn't let them buy"!

Overselling happens when we forget to lock the sale away, and we continue to give more information after they have asked to buy or said "yes". And I bet this has happened to you? You've gone in to buy something, and someone's confused you, and you think, "Now I don't know, so I'm going to think about it and do some more research". So we went somewhere to buy something but left more confused than when we walked in.

So when someone asks to buy or says "yes" to one of your 3 closes, it's a "yes", and if you've got a sale, lock it in! Thank them and do the paperwork! Then, go to the till to get paid! Get the order started! Whatever it takes to lock this sale away while they want it.

For example, if I had just sold a car, the buyer asked about leather seats. That's not overselling because they've asked, but what we do next determines if we oversell. Remember, let's lock this sale away first. So my response would be something like, "Great question. Let me look at that for you, but first, let's get your name on this car you want so we don't lose it. Then, once we lock it in, I'll see what deals I can do for your extras like leather. Is that OK"?

This happened all the time at ReNet with website designs. A new client would get excited about their new website after we had quoted it, and they would start asking about extra pages and ways to display images or graphics. And we wanted to sell them all of it, but the first thing we did was get them locked in. "Tom, let me get you locked in

This is what successful people say, do, and when.

first, it's easy to add on extras as we build your site, but the first thing we need to do is get you scheduled and started". So we'd get their 50% deposit and schedule them into the available time slot and were both committed, and then we looked at the extras. The funny thing is, often, people didn't actually want the extras, but they were interested in understanding how some things worked. And that meant that if we had focused on those things before we locked the sale away, that would have confused them and been overselling.

Overselling is a salesperson's disease, it and it really does exist. When they say "yes", we've got a sale. Lock it away. Your job is done!

Do you Want Fries With That?

Who remembers this from McDonald's? Do you want fries with that?

Did you know this apparently made McDonald's an extra $100,000/year for every register when they introduced it? Yep, it was only about an additional $1 per sale or about $273/per day. McDonald's understood that the best time to sell a man a tie is when he buys a suit.

So after you lock the sale away, now is a great time to ask, "Do you want fries with that"? Someone has just said "yes", they are now in a great mood, and they have just made a great decision to purchase. So Now is the best time to offer a little extra. What's the best time to sell us roof racks or floor mats? Straight after we bought our new car. True?

So we are adding more value to what they have purchased, which is perfect. We're not questioning their purchase or overselling. We ask if they want a few extras with it, which is a natural thing to do. Same as at a restaurant, when they ask if we want any sides with our meals.

Asking someone if they want a tie as they buy a suit should not ruin a sale. People often buy a suit, a shirt, and a tie. They buy a whole set while they are there. In other words, they are in the buying mood, and it's our job to let them buy as much as they want. If we don't, they may spend their money with someone else, so we have a responsibility to the buyer to offer them "what else".

Timing is important, though, and you need to have locked the sale away before asking your extra fries questions, or else it may confuse them. Stick to the initial sale, and get your "yes" answer first to avoid overselling.

When my wife gets her hair cut, the salon has shampoo and treatments she can buy afterwards. At the beauty salon, creams and moisturisers she can buy. At the supermarket, at the cash register, they have all the small items people ad to their trollies at the register. Everyone successful business has its fries with that offer.

What's important is that if they've just bought something from you, they feel they've been able to buy the best package available from you.

When They Negotiate?

Yet it's common practice today for people to negotiate on price.

"What's your best price"? "Can I have a discount"? Blah, Blah, Blah!

But don't panic or get offended. Negotiation is a good thing! They are not asking your competition for the best price. They're asking you! They want your do-it-now reasons. So expect and plan for a negotiation. It's a great situation to be in.

Generally speaking, negotiation means… I am almost there, but I don't understand the value yet. Just give me one more good reason to buy! Negotiation often doesn't mean they want a discount but a little more of something. And when someone asks for a deal, you need to be prepared. It's not good to answer with "No, the price is the price". You don't need to discount, maybe offer a positive call to action, throw in a bonus or put a package together and create a win for them, but refrain from discounting.

You can we tell a poor salesperson from someone who's experienced? Because the poor salesperson discounts their price rather than selling the value. Successful salespeople know the value of their products and services and don't sell on price. Successful salespeople may negotiate because a negotiation means the buyer is ready to buy, but they sell on value propositions. They know that buyers negotiate on price because they have yet to understand the real or actual value to them. So they fulfil that rather than discounting.

A buyer could be just testing you. If someone wants to give me a discount, I will take it, and so will you. So I often ask these same discount questions myself. But I am testing the salesperson to see how they react. It's fun to see some squirm and discount their pricing instead of coming back with excellent reasons to buy. And that's how you can get some fantastic buys.

So negotiating generally means they are ready to buy now. But you should hear them say, "Just give me one or two more reasons why I should buy". So understand that your presentation isn't finished when someone starts haggling over price. So go back a few steps and start delivering FAB again, the benefits of what you've been discussing rather than discounting.

A great practice is acknowledging the offer or question, but then we Business Judo® it with a solution and counteroffer with a further close.

"Scotty, can you do the $5,000 website for a better price"?

"Tom, I can take a few features out for you if you like. Happy to do less and help you save some money if that's what you need, but you like what we have looked at so far, don't you"?

"And Tom, you want that new modern website with those features, don't you"?

"And you want your website to be a priority and completed on time, don't you"?

"So Tom, let's get started"?

See, I acknowledge, but no discounting. And if Tom had said, no, I really need to save $1000 to do the job, then we would have taken some features out. So there is still that option, so I don't lose the sale or client.

Another solution example is, "Tom, I can save you $500 if we put you in the low-priority queue, so your website will be done when there are no others to do in the queue. I am happy to do that if you are in no rush and happy to wait, or do you want your website to be completed next month as we spoke about"?

A package solution example is "Tom. The $5,000 is a great price, but the team has a new image solution that will be $500 extra. We can throw in that as an extra on your website as we need some examples to show others, meaning you will be one of the first in the industry with this on your website. Would you like that instead"?

Or, "Tom, I'd love to discount. However, everything you have asked for is top-notch, with the latest design techniques, and your website will be the best in the area, and that's what you want, isn't it"?

They are some examples of giving them a call to action and why they should buy now and not discounting. This is what you hear when someone starts negotiating on price. They are saying "Yes", but remind me… "Why you", "Why your products", and "Why now"?

Buyers Remorse

Someone says yes, goes away, and we suddenly lose the sale, they need a refund, or the contract gets torn up! Why? What just happened? That's called buyers remorse.

Whether we like it or not, 100% of sales do not mean 100% of them become customers, just like returns at a retail shop.

Buyer's remorse happens for a few reasons.

- We didn't lock the sale away.
- We oversold.
- We were too good a salesperson.
- We didn't let them buy, so they felt sold to.
- Mum/dad/brother/sister talked them out of it when they got home.

This is what successful people say, do, and when.

Buyer's remorse happens more with larger transactions. People say "yes", even sign the contract, then go home, tell the wife, husband, mum or dad and explain what they're buying. Only to be told that they shouldn't be buying it like that! They are told they should be doing this or that instead, or to check more, blah blah blah… So buyers begin to doubt their buying decision and get buyer's remorse.

This is a very, very common situation, and it often happens. You've done it yourself. You've bought something, and you tell someone about it, and they say, "What'd you do that for"? Or someone tells us what they are buying, and we say something similar, like, "Did you look a the other ones? They are better".

So what are some of the things you can do to avoid buyer's remorse?

Firstly, do not sow the seed of buyer's remorse by saying, "If you have any problems, let me know". They will let us know if there are problems, so you don't need to prompt them with negative seeds. We need to avoid buyer's remorse, not encourage it. So we sow positive and proactive seeds instead. Let me explain.

For example, when selling a website to someone, and they just said "yes", the first thing we did was start the buyer on a journey of what happens next, and we do it as soon as we have locked the sale away. Not tomorrow, or next week, now! We try to get their logos, colours, and framework mapped out straight away. By doing this, I am planning that it's too late, no matter what buyer's remorse someone receives. If someone tells them they should have tried their best friend, who is a website designer, it's too late. We are already building their new website for them. Possession is 9/10ths of the law.

This was critical for us at ReNet because often, they already had a website but wanted it upgraded with us. After signing up, they told their current website designer they would no longer have them as their website host. And what do you think happened? Their designer would say things like, "I can do that". So our sales system pre-planned for buyer's remorse in our close. Because we knew this would happen, so why let it happen? Our system was to make sure that the transition into what's next was done ASAP and was seamless. That's our responsibility, not theirs.

Someone bought, so the very next thing you need to do to eliminate is buyer's remorse. Now positively lock the sale away, reaffirm their decision with positive actions like "let's get started" and "looking forward to getting this built", and sow these seeds straight after the sale. Right now, in the closing stage of your system, that's the best time to be effective and eliminate any doubt and influence from other people when they get home.

Brochures Won't Close

So, business cards, brochures and websites do NOT sell, and they DO NOT close for you either. So, when you give a brochure, think of it as a goodbye, as 99% of leads and opportunities will be cold and gone. Who wants to lose 99% of their opportunities?

"But Scotty, I have had people buy from a brochure". I am sure eventually, someone will buy from one. After all, sales is a numbers game. But if you want to increase your strike rate, save your money!

Some salespeople love brochures because they haven't been trained to use their closes. So they believe a buyer will go home, look at the brochure and think, "This brochure is unreal. I need to buy". Unfortunately, the percentage of buyers that do this is minimal. How often have you taken a brochure, then put it straight into the bin at home, and many times without even reading it further? We do it a lot, don't we?

A bird in the hand is worth two in the bush. So brochure giving is one of the worst sales systems ever. A salesperson gets to the end of their presentation, and they provide a brochure as their close. And by giving them a brochure as a close, the salesperson avoided having to ask a closing question and just gave them the "I'll think about it" strategy.

So brochure giving could also be called "close" avoidance. The fear of asking for the sale. That's why some provide a brochure and then get

This is what successful people say, do, and when.

their phone number as part of their system, then maybe phone them up with, "I gave you a brochure last week. Do you have any more questions"? And that system is a terrible use of brochures.

I have had a few salespeople I have trained from the print industry, so they get all their print material cheap, so they start handing out these everywhere only to wonder why people aren't buying their services. It's because they aren't selling. They are brochure-dropping, which may work for $9.95 pizzas but not for sales.

So what do you do when someone asks for your business card or brochure? And they do, don't they?

Here's the system I followed. I didn't have business cards or brochures. So when someone asked, "I'd like to think about it, do you have a brochure"? My reply was, "We don't have them"? Followed with something like, "And was the website or CRM you wanted to think about"? In other words, I redirected them back into the presentation again rather than letting them go back into the cold zone. And that's what brochure giving does. It allows people to go cold again instead of keeping our conversation going.

The rule of thumb is that when someone asks you for your business cards or brochures, you lose the sale. When leads say, "I want to think about it. Do you have a brochure"? While that may seem a hot response, it's not! 99.9% of the time, it just means that they will go cold, and the brochure goes in the bin when they get home. So work out strategies for when this happens. What can you put into your systems when this happens? How can you get back to what's important? If they are seriously interested, then now is the time to discuss it. And if they are not, then save your money.

Brochures mean more work and fewer results. Brochures will not close deals, and they do not go home with your buyers and continue your conversation.

Use the systems in this book instead. That's how you will make more sales and make more money.

This is what successful people say, do, and when.

This is Not a Close

"Are you sure"?

This has to be one of the worst responses I have ever heard salespeople say. But, of course, they are sure. Instead, it's questioning their intelligence. And we never question their intelligence!

"Are you sure"?

"Yes, I'm sure, and I'm sure I don't want to deal with you"!

Remember the three reasons we ask questions and the golden rule? "Are you sure" breaks all the rules. Salespeople don't mean to question the buyer's intelligence. I believe they asked this to fill in time, to give the salesperson thinking time to rebut them with a response.

Yet, I heard this repeatedly during training, which means it was said in real life.

Avoiding this is as simple as training, practising your closes, and knowing what to say when someone wants to think about it. Perfect practice makes perfect.

Another way I avoided this was by using the appointment after the appointment system. When an agent wanted to think about it when I didn't get a "yes", I'd set up our next meeting. "I'd like to think about it" "OK, I'm available Tuesday or Thursday at two o'clock, do either of those work for you"? Another was a reason to come back "I'd like to think about it" "OK, let me get some more information and come back to you. I'm available Tuesday or Thursday at two o'clock, do either of those work for you"?

"Are you sure"? This has no place in sales! Of course, they are sure, and we support them. Never question their intelligence.

Working Pipeline

So what happens when we don't get a "yes" answer?

This is what successful people say, do, and when.

We've talked as much as possible, but we are still not getting a "yes" or "no". They are still in the middle and opportunity third in the Business of Thirds® system. Then we put them into our pipeline. So a maybe is OK too. It just means we have more work to do if we want their business.

Most salespeople talk up all the sales they have in their pipeline. But sales in our pipeline do not pay the bills. Back in the insurance days, we didn't have a pipeline. It was a yes or no situation; a maybe was just a no. Our strike rate was terrible if someone said to come back in a few days so they could think about it. Although I always followed up, I learnt quickly that a sale was mostly lost once I left, so it was better not to walk away or walk away with a firm no or try one more time while I was there.

But a pipeline may have a place in your system. It did at ReNet. Let me explain.

A lead is saying, "I'll think about it". What did I do in that situation? I've done my presentation, and they still want to think about it. I use the appointment after the appointment, or meeting after the meeting system as my working pipeline and schedule my next meeting. And that works perfectly. Embracing the meeting after the meeting as part of the system takes the pressure off them.

This is my working pipeline, so what I do next is map out a future pipeline for them too. Then I listened for more clues, and many people immediately gave me more information. Why? I'd just taken the pressure off them, so they opened up a little more. They would say things like, "I'd like to think about size or colour". In other words, they'd now tell me more reasons. Then I can continue to talk about their reasons and answer them now too, and sometimes that would help close the sale there and then. Or I'd continue to sow seeds for our future meeting with more information, depending on where I thought their 4 levels of the Human Mind were.

Another way to work my pipeline was to ensure they end up in my warm zone, that's our CRM and contact database too, so they receive emails from us from time to time. Because if someone wanted to buy six months ago and they come in today and purchased, I'm still going to be happy. Very happy!

Some people do fall into the category of not being ready right now. The worst thing we can do at that point is disrespecting them for their decision to wait. They like us and our products and services, but it's not today for whatever reason.

So pipeline them, work your pipeline correctly and create an action plan. If we want their business, then it is our responsibility to keep them interested.

This is what successful people say, do, and when.

SYSTEM 17

Follow Up

I was in the fire brigade for 8 years and am trained in advanced CPR. Our training told us that with CPR, we keep going until they recover, or we are exhausted, or someone else turns up and takes over. A sale is the same; buyers are not dead until they say "no" or buy elsewhere. Then, if there is a chance with a lead, I will keep doing follow-up until they either buy from me, I'm exhausted, or they buy with someone else. And that's what successful salespeople do.

"I give people three chances, or they are out"! This was what someone told me once. But seriously, what a tosser! If someone wants to become a client and spend money with me next year, then that's OK by me. And, how good is it when you get sales this year because of what you did last year? Too easy, hey?

> *It's not often you get a second chance at another first impression!*

So your follow-up is your secret sauce. It's not often that you get a second chance at another first impression! So getting your follow-up right has got to be one of your most effective systems, and this one system alone is what sets high achievers apart from others. It's amazing how much gold there is to be had in an effective follow-up system. It's out there, and it's yours for the taking.

This is what successful people say, do, and when.

So follow-up is also part of your immediate sales system with anyone in the warm zone. For example, my wife and I recently went to a restaurant, and a QR code for ordering food was on the table. COVID has introduced many things, and this is one of them. I had never been there before and had yet to learn what was good or bad on the menu or what I even wanted. After a short time, we were still determining if we even wanted to stay for dinner. Then the waiter came and served us. He saw we hadn't taken to the QR code and saw our big white flag, so he followed up with us to make sure we were OK. He then took our order. He also continued serving us or following up throughout the night, so we stayed drinking, eating, and enjoying ourselves for a few hours. His immediate follow-up paid them back 10 fold.

So never throw the baby away with the bathwater. Some people want you to help them make their buying decision, and if their business is worth it, then it's worth investing in your follow-up systems. Yet many people avoid it. "If they want it, they'll ask"! Which is true. But successful people don't wait. They make things happen.

4 Levels of the Human Mind

Many leads that don't buy today are still open-minded. Many haven't purchased with the competition yet, which is good news as many procrastinate to buy. But they are still open and very much warm leads, so the way you do your follow-up is always very suggestive and open-minded.

Be sensitive and supportive. Don't interrogate with lots of questions or try to close them. The purpose of follow-up is to keep their minds and the journey open. Or one way to look at it is that we are still at the introduction or presentation stage of the cycle. We're still building their confidence and belief in us and our products. Then when they are ready, you want them to buy from you, not your competition. So keep them open and in your warm zone for as long as possible.

This is what successful people say, do, and when.

Beat Your Competition

One of the reasons follow-up is the most effective way to differentiate yourself from the competition is that this is the only part of the sales and business cycle where you are in complete control.

What does being in control mean?

Well, it's because you now have more control than when they were first a lead. You now know the buyer, things like their hot spots, pain or needs. You may not understand why they still haven't said "yes" or why they want to think about it. But when you spoke to them the first time, you didn't know anything about them, but now you do. Now you know more about them now than you did before, don't you?

Follow-up still has lots of action and reaction. Think of it as though you are starting again every time you do. For example, when selling big ticket items, you can prepare and create a list of everything the customer wants and how you will solve their problem because you now know these. You've had a conversation with them, which has given you this position of power: you're now following up with phone calls, direct messages, or emails with extra knowledge you can use. So for the first time, you can start with what to say, do, and when.

In reverse, they were in control when they first came to us and asked us questions. But we follow up with them to increase our strike rate and separate ourselves from the competition. It's now our turn. And whether we're following up three, four, or five times, at every point of the follow-up, we are in control of what happens. Mostly, when we follow up, we go back into our introduction and presentation mode. Hopefully, they haven't said "yes" to anyone yet, so we always go back to our presentation and remember that follow-up is not your close.

When done well, your follow-up will put you in a position of strength, not the other way around. And that's why follow-up is the secret sauce. Plan it out and follow your system, and that's how buyers will prefer you over your competition.

White Flags

Think of a white flag as a lead or prospect waving a giant white flag for help. They want to surrender to your services and get your advice.

For example, it's a great sign when they follow up with us by themselves and ask us more questions before we get the chance to follow up with them. It means they are interested, and you have done great with your presentation and pipeline, and well done! They are waving a giant white flag and asking for more reasons to buy.

Someone with a white flag is in the buying mood. And they have yet to spend their money. But some people need a little more to say "yes", so this could be one of the easiest sales you ever make. But rookie salespeople think white flags are such a pain. And this can be the case, and I know some people seem to window shop all the time and never buy, but they are in your warm zone and not in your competition's warm zone, so it's your responsibility to make things happen.

For example, when my wife and I were in the restaurant I mentioned earlier, wanting a good night, we could have easily had one drink and then gone somewhere else, but the waiter saved us.

Or when considering upgrading my car, I'd often visit the dealers to check out the new cars. I am ready and wanted to, but I just didn't get tipped over by anyone to go ahead. So I didn't buy one, and they didn't get a sale either. The thing is that I didn't go to the florist shop, boat dealers or RV centre. I went to car dealers because I was interested. And we all do that. We research and shop around for what interests us, sometimes talking to someone 3 or 4 times researching. But when we do that, we are waving a giant white flag. White flags are us looking for reasons to spend now, and your buyers are the same.

So the white flags are ready to buy and often only need one more thing to tip them over positively. All you have to do is help them before someone else does.

Reasons

Restaurants and cafes have been doing this for years, we sit down, and well-trained staff ask us if we want to start with a drink. If so, they will take the order and let us know what's next, often that they will be back with the food menu soon. They continually create reasons to keep helping us spend more on drinks or desserts while we are at the table. They understand that every extra dollar spent on every table is worth it. So good restaurants train staff for effective and immediate follow-up, reasons to make it easy for us to spend a bit more with them. And if the staff are good, they can instantly be rewarded with tips too.

The secret is your ability to have something they want to know, a genuine reason and expectation of what's next. That's your follow-up.

For big-ticket items, I spoke about creating a meeting after the meeting. They are in the middle third if we don't get a yes or no. If we still want their business, we need to schedule the next meeting before they leave.

The perfect follow-up is for us to create reasons for our follow-up as we finish our presentation. For example, we get them some more information, research, check on stock, and create reasons for our next call. Say something like, "I'll get you some more information. Is that all right"? Or "I will phone you back in a few days. Is that OK"? Most people will say "yes" to both of those questions. You are going in to bat for them; generally, people love that you will look after them.

This system is also a test close. We don't want to do work for someone who doesn't want to buy, do we? So it's a qualifier because if they say, "It's OK, we'll get back to you", you know they may be cold. So there's not much point flogging a dead horse, is there? We can then add them to our email database so that system can do follow-up for us, or we can schedule a call at a later date that we make, even without reason. But if they respond positively, you have reason to invest more time into them as warm to hot leads. And warm leads are better than cold ones!

The good news is that while we are creating reasons for our follow-up, they generally will qualify themselves too. And that means they may even start the conversation again, and we obtain more information that we can sometimes use right now to close the sale and not later because we have created an environment that has opened people up to tell us more.

For example, as a car salesperson, "I'll get back to you with some research on colour availability. Quickly, what's your preference"? "Red"? "OK, although I believe we have a red one being delivered next month, I can check on that now if you like"? See how the extra information can sometimes make it possible to continue the sale now by combining some test closes with the additional information?

Either way, our follow-up gives us control over what information we go back with. And sometimes we have to create them, for example, as a car salesperson. "Is it OK to call you when the new model arrives"? Something like that. We make a reason to contact them.

When you give great follow-up by phone or email, you're doing what you said you would do in the first place. You organised it, and now you are delivering on your promise. And that's how you keep your follow-up momentum going and beat your competition. You continually follow up until such a time as they've got enough confidence, belief and trust that you're the person they want to do business with, or they say no!

So when you follow up with them, they will generally make time for you. "Hey Tom, good news! I now have what you are looking for"? Typically, Tom will want that, so he will make time to talk to you again. So now you are off and running again with your presentation.

Follow-up is very rewarding when you have good reasons to do it.

Sow Seeds

Whenever I end a conversation, I always plant the seed that we will stay in touch. And how do I do that? By saying precisely that. "Stay in touch". We must leave the door open for them to contact us anytime.

This is what successful people say, do, and when.

Seed examples;

- I'll stay in touch.
- You stay in touch.
- I will get back to you soon.
- Talk soon.
- Looking forward to our next catch-up.

Use closing statements to the effect that we are there for them next. These are all positive ways you finish a conversation and sow the seeds that make people feel comfortable about either of us following up.

Do not use the reverse of these positive seed examples, the terrible "let me know if you have any questions"? Or "Let me know if you're interested". All these say I don't care about your business.

So who's in control here? We are, and we want them to know we are here to support them. We want them to know they can trust us to be the person that's going to deliver what we promise. And how we do that is by leaving the door open and staying in touch, so when we say it, it's a genuine statement and one we can honour.

So keep people in your warm zone, understand how your sales system works, and seed your follow-up. "Stay in touch".

As Second Impressions

You never get a second chance at another first impression. Yes, you do!

So here's the flip. Most people think the follow-up is at the end of the sale, as it's after we've done our presentation and tried to close. But the follow-up is often actually our introduction. "So how does that work"? I'm glad you asked! Let me explain.

Remember that every transaction has an introduction, transaction, and close? So that means we get to do our introduction again when we follow up. So you must do another introduction, starting with an

This is what successful people say, do, and when.

assumption that they are back to being open-minded buyers whenever you speak to someone again.

Let's imagine someone meeting someone new outside of work. Most people ask, "So what do you do"? They respond with their mini introduction or elevator pitch. Some may respond with something like, "That's exciting"? The typical reaction is to think that they have a hot lead, so they will go on about what they do. But don't. A networking event, BBQ, or anything out of the warm zone is the wrong place to build up our buying environment. So what do we do? We schedule a second follow-up and introduction. Say something like a test close, "I'd love to explain more about what I do. Can we catch up next week"? So we are now doing our introduction as a follow-up to our 60-second introduction. In fact, you haven't even started. And your follow-up has now become your second chance at another first impression.

Let me give you a funny story. I was at the garbage tip at the end of 2001 as I was renovating, simply dropping off the garbage. A work truck pulled up beside me, sign-written with North Coast Chemicals. I had never met this guy and had no idea if he was a worker or the owner. But at the time, I was building websites to make some money. Anyway, my conversation with this guy went something like this, "hey, I've been meaning to come and see you. I am so glad you pulled up". He said, "Why"? I said, "I want to talk to you about your website, as I have a few other clients already near you". He responded, "Sure, can you come in and see me next week? Any afternoon is fine". He then gave me his card. BOOM! And that was a true story, and I started again, and yes, he did build a website with me. So that trip to the garbage tip made me money.

So following up with someone that is not a client yet is still a potential buyer, even if it's the 5th time. They are still a lead; with every lead, you get a second chance at another first impression. Think about it. This is how you use meetings and introductions as part of a follow-up system when you meet someone to get to where you want to be. First, you must get into a warm zone and have a proper constructive conversation allowing your second chance meeting.

It's Not Your Close

"Scotty, I am following up to see if you are ready to buy"?

Wording like this is a close and not a follow-up. Yet I have seen these kinds of follow-up emails plenty in my coaching.

I am trying to say that if you use direct closing questions in your follow-up, there's a high probability of getting a negative reaction. If I were ready to buy, I would have already responded, right? So when someone asks about doing business with us as a follow-up, they've asked a dumb question. Plus, it's a question that breaks all the question rules.

Effective follow-up is your system for keeping people open-minded, not closing them. Follow-up is not your close!

The Best Follow Up

The best follow-up is one that is prepared.

And what is the best follow-up system? Is it an email or a phone call?

Well, it's whatever you need to do to follow up. My preference for a follow-up is face-to-face or belly-to-belly. I know that's not always practical. But I try to either make time to see someone or phone them. And with so much reliance on emails, it's amazing how effective a face-to-face call can be.

Also, many follow-ups are done by email or direct messages. And the benefit of a written follow-up is that you get the time to prepare your words properly because you have the time and are in control. But emails are a lot colder, aren't they? They can be dry, and a word or line may be misread or taken out of context. But you are in control of this part, and if you're going to be in control, you can do your follow-up the way you feel the most comfortable.

Follow-up can happen any place we interact and have a conversation with someone. Sometimes, we can comment on social media as a part of our constructive follow-up. But the most constructive follow-up is face-to-face and, if possible, in the warm zone.

This is what successful people say, do, and when.

Remember that you're building up the 4 Levels of the Human Mind as you take people on your know, like and trust journey.

Otherwise, it doesn't matter how you prefer to do your follow-up. Practise and train for it. It's up to you how you do it, but not losing people is the best follow-up system of all.

Expect It and Beat Your Competition

Remember, if you're worth it and you can prove it, you'll get paid it. And follow-up allows you to prove you are better than your competitors.

Where a lot of my competition fell over was in their follow-up. We took advantage of this because it was part of our system. See, much of your competition generally doesn't have this as a strength, and some even think that following up with leads is a pain. But, if you know and use the Business of Thirds® system, you know there is an opportunity layer of 60%. So using this means that using your follow-up as part of your system is how you often beat your competition. I did.

For example, if I was a Ford salesperson, and someone really wanted a new car and came to my dealership but didn't buy it straight away, there's probably a big chance they will look at other dealers too and shop around. So what set's me apart from the other dealers? It would be my follow-up!

The best system is to expect to follow up and know that it is part of your system. With big-ticket items, customers wait to say yes, and they need to go through the 4 Levels of the Human Mind, especially if they're going to become customers rather than just a sale.

So like a restaurant, a car dealer or us at ReNet, expect follow-up and create a system for it so you make more.

Don't Bug Them

"But Scotty, I don't want to bug them"?

Bugging clients may happen, but not from you!

You want to deliver an effective follow-up. You will know what to say, do, and when if you've used all your systems. Like what their hot spots, pain, or needs are. And you ask the right questions, and you have sowed the seeds. Then guess what? You're not going to bug them. And when done well, they expect you to follow up, and they will be disappointed when you don't. (Have you had that happen to you?)

They may have been interested a week ago, but we followed up this week, and things have changed. Probably not our fault. Remember, in the Business of Thirds®, 60% can go either way depending on what happens, so we can expect some to drop off and others to come back.

Follow-up is not bugging leads. On the contrary, it adds extra value to the customer. We give them what they want in 60% of cases, so that's not annoying. But if you feel like you're bugging customers, you need to do more things earlier in your systems. For example, a waiter in a restaurant is not bugging us when they check in on us to see if we need anything more. Generally, we appreciate NOT being left alone. And that's the same with big ticket items. They expect it, and it's not bugging them. They expect your expertise.

If I use a car dealer example and a new model is being released. I'd look for potential customers in my database (as I'd created a list of people with everything they wanted). And what do you think they would say if I sent them a message or phoned them about the new release or the special limited edition? Of course, they would say, "That's awesome". So that doesn't mean they'd buy. But that's not bugging them. It's informing them and keeping them warm for when they are ready. See the difference?

So when done well, buyers want us to keep them in our warm zone. I bet you love it when businesses keep you in their warm zone when you're interested, and someone treats you like you're important, don't you?

So your system needs to have people appreciating you because you treat them as important too, and they won't see it as you bugging them.

This is what successful people say, do, and when.

The Best Follow Up Line

Generally, with our follow-up, we already know what to say, do, and when because of everything we previously did.

But what if we can't remember, or we are prospecting our old database, and we look through our old contacts or cancelled clients list? Sometimes we are in a situation of not knowing as much as we should. So what is the best way to follow up when this happens?

This is one of the best lines I've ever used for general or blind follow-up. It's effortless. So subtle yet designed to open the conversational door again. I'll send a very brief message asking, "How's it all going"? And that's all I ask. Now they are open to answering with whatever they want to talk about. Even if people didn't answer, that's OK by me. But it's incredible how often this line works and will get a conversation started again.

What I don't talk about is what we spoke about last time. I bet you think I should, but I don't want to direct their thinking (yet). I want them to feel comfortable starting another conversation again, and that's all for now.

The only thing better than that question is finding a genuine reason to start a conversation again. Social media is excellent for this too. For example, let's say I've seen something on their social media, and I then follow up with a positive statement about it. Like, "Well done on winning that award", "excellent photo you posted", "Congratulations on the new job", and "10 years at ABC, well done"! These positive statements almost always get a positive "thank you" reaction. And then I follow with, "And how's it all going". So I am not selling, but I am showing genuine interest in them and their work. Follow-up is essential in your sales system. If someone wants to spend money on what you have, then why not you?

So plan, prepare and practice follow-up. It's what successful people do!

This is what successful people say, do, and when.

If someone wants to buy today and you spoke to them last year, then that's perfect.

SYSTEM 18

Marketing

How many marketing experts does it take to screw in a light bulb? None, as they have automated it! Very funny, and it's true. Automating marketing makes sense so we can spend more time protecting and on the front line making things happen.

"Scotty, I'm busy doing lots of marketing but not making any sales"! Me: "OK, so how many prospecting calls have you made today? Or this week or this month"? Them: "None"! Me: "Then how do you expect to get paid"? The problem today is that many people do marketing thinking it's selling!

Marketing is not the problem. It's part of the sales cycle and is essential for many reasons, especially lead generation. The good news is that marketing has to be one of the easiest systems to learn and leverage. Generally, everybody does marketing, especially on social media, and there is so much free information about how to market better. Therefore allow me to be succinct here, and rather than how to do actual marketing, I'll talk about how I used these sales systems for marketing with a $0 budget at ReNet to achieve sales consistently.

Although I have trained many people who dedicate so much time and spend a lot of money on advertising and marketing but still need to make money. It appears to me that marketing and thinking it's selling may be a modern-day issue.

The good news is that you can leverage all the systems in this book to succeed with your marketing. And that means making more sales. And your marketing approach can be more relaxed. Let me explain.

4 Levels of the Human Mind

Marketing builds confidence in your brand and can be utilised with people at any of the 4 levels. Firstly, marketing, it's to open people's minds and bring them into our warm zone, even if they are already existing clients. In other words, you are building confidence and belief in people to have a conversation with them (a presentation).

For example, at ReNet, if someone in real estate wanted a website, CRM, XML, etc. Then I needed to tell them what we did so they would think of us. And that included people in every zone, cold, warm or hot. In other words, we did marketing for non-clients, our prospects, and our existing clients. As I said, I grew a company with very little marketing and an actual budget of $0, so our email list and CRM were gold. Although, now and then, I did throw an ad into a magazine or sponsor events because of the discounted pricing offered to us.

Today, with social media, marketing is even easier to keep opening people's minds. We can share photos, docs, and videos and interview people. Sharing stories and content to remind people who we are, what we offer, and how we solve their problems. And that's perfect for opening people's minds, which is great. But from my experience, marketing will not replace you in building up people's confidence and belief.

Marketing is an integral part of the cycle, but today many people put too much weight on marketing, and all they do is marketing, yet they are making little money. That's because marketing is at the top of their sales funnel, but then they forget about the actual selling. So while I like the sales funnel system, I believe sales is also a cycle, and the business and sales cycle draws people into the centre and your hot zone. So I believe it's better to actively draw people in rather than hope they will fall out of the bottom of a marketing funnel. There are six stages to your sales system, not just one.

Marketing is proactive. You open people's minds to get a positive reaction, build confidence and belief, and then you make things happen.

This is what successful people say, do, and when.

Marketing is Not Selling

You're the salesperson! You can't expect your business card, brochure, website, or social media to do your selling for you. Of course, this can happen, especially as you build up confidence and belief from people, but marketing is getting people to talk to you so you can do the selling.

If you've got a special offer and something's discounted, people may want to buy it straight from the marketing. Think cheap Tuesday at the local pizza shop or end of the season in retail. A give with a discount price option in marketing does have a place, like cheap and quick sales. Marketing a discount could even be your Trojan Horse or FAD. But giving discounts is not selling. Anyone can discount. And if you put prices on your marketing, then we are also putting in a close. A buyer will then decide based on your price and not FAB. And with big ticket items, you don't want that!

You want to make more profitable sales, not discount or give stuff away. So the more you can close profitable deals, the better. Yet I meet many people relying on their marketing to sell or to sell for them.

Marketing is for opening people's minds so we can transition them to clients. To do that, we need to have our sales conversation with them and do our presentation. So our marketing goal is to attract them to our buying environment so we can begin the sales process.

So selling is different from marketing, marketing is important and can motivate people to make a decision, but marketing does not sell. You do! Marketing does not replace you as a salesperson!

4 Gives, Then an Ask

My wife once asked me, "Have you run out of things to post on LinkedIn yet"? I said, "I haven't even started"!

I hear people say, "But if I share all my secrets, then nobody will need to pay me"? And while that has some truth, the reality is that if sharing a few things about what they know is ALL their knowledge, then there are more significant issues here if that's all they know.

So what's a perfect system in marketing is to position yourself as an expert? This is the system I teach; 4 gives, then an ask. This system works excellently in the real estate industry. Let me explain. Imagine a real estate agent knocking on someone's door and asking, "Do you want to sell your house"? The answer would probably be "no", as most people are not selling. So rather than asking if they want to sell, they ask, "Would you like a free property valuation"? Or "Would you like to be kept up on market valuations"? And most people do. Homeowners love knowing how much capital gain they have made on their homes. So real estate agents work this system of giving before asking. Sharing knowledge to create touchpoints and build up know, like, and trust. So the system being used here is that they give before they ask. But an agent working this system knows they need 4 gives, then an ask.

For example, boxers use a jib, jib, then jab system. And a fisherman gives burley to stir up the fish. So experts share knowledge. The thing is that knowledge is everywhere. So what people pay you for is to help them use your knowledge. And when people think about getting help, they think of who the expert is. And that is when this system works. Who has been helping them already?

Although, when I was selling insurance, we cold-called, and there was no marketing, no gives, just a straight-up ask. It was very direct. With ReNet, it was much the same when I prospected. But when I was prospecting, it was the early days of ReNet and the internet. I also delivered free training and sharing of knowledge as part of my prospecting system, and my 4 gives, then an ask.

Today, with social media, it's more like 20 gives then an ask. In fact, it could even be argued that it's almost all gives and no asks in marketing.

In other words, marketing is a great way to share our knowledge and what people what to know first. We build up the 4 Levels of the Human Mind as we position ourselves as an expert in our industry.

But even so, it's easier today than ever to position yourself as an expert in social media and the internet. Sharing expertise in your blogs, videos, reports, posts, and podcasts is easy. And the more you give with marketing, the more you get back.

As Follow Up

At ReNet, marketing had a lot to do with follow-up. Meaning when I did a presentation, and they fell into my pipeline and bottom or middle third with the Business of Thirds®, then my marketing helped as my follow-up. I didn't rely on this as the follow-up, but staying on top of their mind is essential. Remember, the middle third of people will go either way, depending on what happens.

Marketing helps the 60% of opportunities in sales. Timing is essential, so use the Rule of 100™ to schedule a trial of follow-up marketing. If someone was interested in our products and services last year, we are still happy for them to buy now. We want them to buy from us and not the competition when they are ready, right?

Let me give you an example. At ReNet, our retention of clients was very high. We also didn't have contracts, so nobody was forced to stay due to signing one. But some people did cancel, with about a 3-4% per year churn. The thing is, I knew that agents cancelled for the same reason they started. An interesting stat that was very interesting is that, on average, about 14% of sales at ReNet every year were clients that had previously cancelled for whatever reason but came back. Real estate agents get into a franchise and then get out. They get into partnerships and then get out. Our Business Judo® was also to ensure they were kept updated with marketing and our latest information, making it easy for them to return.

It's much easier to sell to someone who has previously spent money with us than someone who is completely cold. They returned because we reminded them of their know, like, and trust in us. And when they cancelled, we knew some would come back, so we planned for it. And that is where marketing to our database worked. We scheduled emails to

This is what successful people say, do, and when.

remind them about all the good things ReNet was doing in the real estate industry. And it worked. And today, it's even easier, as we all have social media we can leverage and our email list.

Sometimes when we get busy, it's easy for some of our buyers to fall through the cracks. Remember the Mercedes Benz dealer? He chose to look after someone buying two cars instead of me. And I can't blame him. And when we are busy, it's the same. The point is that marketing can act as your safety net. An additional form of follow-up so less people drop out of your zones and your marketing and sales strategy is to keep them in your buying environment.

Golden Email

At ReNet, our primary system for marketing was the same as what real estate agents paid us for, emails to our email lists. I built my own proprietary emarketing software, we used it, and agents paid for it too. As a result, ReNet had 45,000 real estate emails, plus the real estate agents had over 2.5 million contacts in the CRM who wanted to receive market updates from their local real estate agents. That's a lot of emails going out daily, and you can't do that with Outlook.

Building your database of names and email addresses is essential to your sales system. If you have a small number of clients, you can even use a spreadsheet, just as long as you have a list and do something about it. There are even some free or very cost-effective solutions, and with a small email list, you can even use your email software, like Outlook. But emails to people who want your information continues to prove an excellent marketing strategy.

Email marketing is about constant contact, communication, and conversation with buyers, using emails as another touch point. So you need to keep the buyer warm when you have had a touch point. And that's your responsibility to do that.

Today, social media sites do cool things with people who have had a touch point with your posts. They know who has done that, and then you can target market people down the tiniest of micro-actions. And

This is what successful people say, do, and when.

that's good marketing intelligence, but social media sites keep that intelligence for themselves. They do not give you names and addresses so you can prospect them. Instead, they own all the data and want you to spend money with them.

So that's why you build up your own email list. Because it is yours, you own it as an asset, and you can manage it. At ReNet, I invested in building our email lists, as it was worth it. Sometimes we did this manually. For example, we'd pick a warm or hot zone, then search for new real estate offices and add them to our CRM because it was worth the time it took to build our list.

The point of building your email database is to take advantage of opportunities when you are busy and grow a foundation layer of people you can market to as part of your system and cycle. Whether that's because they've come into your warm zone and have yet to become a client or they are existing clients already. Keeping people updated by email works. It's amazing how many people love to receive your updates from time to time.

Over the years of ReNet, our email list was our most important marketing. First, we built up our database of people that were potential clients and then used it as part of our sales system. We then taught our client agents to build up their lists and do exactly the same, and their email lists worked for them too, and I am sure they will work for you too.

Business Judo® It.

Business Judo® is perfect for marketing. Business Judo® is PMA, collaboration, leveraging, win-win-win and networking, which always got us the best results in marketing. For example, at ReNet, one of our marketing systems was for validation, and we used a third person. Let me explain.

Before we had social media marketing, we had viral marketing. Viral marketing is not when we talk about our product. It's when someone else talks about and says how awesome our products are. And today,

This is what successful people say, do, and when.

people have made millions from being social media influencers. Why? Because viral marketing still works.

Think sponsorship and endorsements. Why did Nike pay Michael Jordan millions each year to throw basketballs and wear Nike shoes? Because people bought Nike to be like him?

So you can use that same system in your marketing too. Validation from someone else in your marketing works unreal. And ReNet's go-to when marketing was to send out information based on clients' success stories. Prospects don't want to know how ReNet is. They want to know that our clients are succeeding by using our products. So that's what we did.

Using Business Judo® for our marketing did two things. Firstly, it created inference and validation to generate leads. That inference was great for the cold zone to open people's minds and, in the warm zone, to remind people who we are. And in the HOT zone to see what other clients were doing and for client retention. Secondly, it extended our relationship with the client that we promoted. See how that's perfect Business Judo®?

You've seen this yourself when the approval and the validation of others influence people. And that's why we use inference in every phase of the sales cycle, and marketing is one of the best.

Use Business Judo® and with a third person whenever you can to validate your products and services. Prospects love it.

SYSTEM 19

Leads

"I just watched an awesome movie. You should watch it".

"Had the best dinner in that restaurant. You should go".

"Had an unreal holiday. You would love it too".

When someone refers business to us, it's much easier, hey?

Why? Referred buyers are generally the easiest sales. Because referral buyers are warmed up by someone they know! It's so much easier when someone comes to you and asks, "My friend has your products. Can you tell me more"? A warm lead like this is gold, and your success rate on these is much higher. But in sales, it's your job to create warm leads too. Anytime someone comes from the cold into your warm zone, it's a buyer; if you don't get a sale, it's a missed opportunity. Every lead is part of your numbers game. If you spoke to 100 people, you want many of those to turn into clients. True?

Yet lead management is one of the forgotten trades today. We all agree that leads are great when they come to us, but when was the last time you verbally asked someone for a lead? Like "Do you know anyone who would also be interested (in your products)"? If I were to start a business again today, I would start with leads. I would begin by asking everyone if they knew anyone that may be interested in what I was doing. While we are at it, if you know someone who would like to improve their sales knowledge or make more money, please send them to the System 1357® website, and they can buy a signed copy of this book too. And if you do, I thank you very much. It's appreciated more than you can know.

This is what successful people say, do, and when.

SELL MORE MAKE MORE - The Best Sales Systems Ever!

You probably think that not all businesses can use lead generation. But I believe they ALL can. Let's use a cafe as an example. If I were to open a cafe, I'd have two options. 1. Open the shop and what for customers (what most people do), or 2. Drive business to me with lead generation. Now try to think about what you could do if this were you. What would you do to start and build a cafe and generate leads? Let me give three examples of driving business or being proactive instead of reactive and waiting for business.

1. Walk to neighbouring shops in the area and let them know I have opened and what I am doing, then invite them in for a coffee. Better still, I'd offer to bring them a coffee.

2. If I had no customers, I'd stand out the front and be warm and welcoming, so people would come in and then make them comfortable to stay and become return customers.

3. Put on some first-week or opening specials. People love a good deal and want to try new things. So I'd let them.

Then, as people entered my cafe, I would make them feel welcomed and appreciated. And I am sure you would too.

So I took this photo I took in Melbourne, Australia July 2022. This is different from the cafe that turned me away at 6:30 am. Notice that the

This is what successful people say, do, and when.

cafe on the left is busy, clients are inside and out, yet the cafe on the right is empty inside and out. Why? Who knows, but more importantly, what's the shop on the right doing about it? I sat across from these two cafes for 30+ minutes, and the cafe on the right stayed empty. I'd be doing something proactive to build leads if it were me. But I watched the five staff standing around doing very little. What would you do if it was your cafe?

"Look after the pennies and the pounds look after themselves".

> **Look after your leads, and sales look after themselves!**

So lead generation is a deliberate and intentional system. We can sit around all day waiting for leads or be proactive and make them. Don't wait for them if you need them! And when someone enters our buying environment, we ensure they feel welcome and that it is a friendly, warm environment for them. Why let people leave our environment only to see them spend their money with someone else?

4 levels of the Human Mind

Firstly, let's examine what people think when they are a lead. Where are they at on the 4 levels?

Anytime someone enters our warm zone and environment, they are a lead, true? But generating warm or referral leads is the true context of generating leads instead of waiting for them. It's the deliberate and intentional act of being proactive, not reactive. Either way, make sure you make the most of your leads regardless of where they come from, warm or not.

When people walk into a store, they know they are entering an environment. Sometimes they are intentional and need or want something, sometimes not. But the store they entered is of interest. If you were interested in flowers, that's a shop you'd go to, not the car dealer. And no one goes to the car dealership to buy flowers either, do they? So anytime someone enters your warm zone, they are open, and there is interest. It may be a passing or strong interest, but they are your lead, and all leads go on a journey through the 4 Levels of the Human Mind.

Regardless of where a lead comes from, they always come out of your cold and into your warm zone. And they want us to listen to their problems, pain, or needs. And that's how we take our leads on a journey from open to confident, and the better we get at the journey, the more successful transactions we make. We meet them where they are mentally and take them on a confidence and belief journey.

On the other hand, when we can get a warm referral lead, our job is half done as their confidence is built up faster because they already have been sown a seed of confidence and belief in them about us and our products from the referrer.

So it's great when someone comes to you as a warm buyer, as they are always open-minded or better. However, unlike when I was cold calling, they were always closed-minded. Remember, it's not until confidence is built that a transaction happens. So ultimately, if you want to make a successful transaction, it's your responsibility to take your buyers on their journey of the 4 Levels of the Human Mind to achieve that.

Prioritise Leads

My wife hates it when I do this. If I don't feel the love when I enter a business, I will walk out and take my money elsewhere, cafes, restaurants, mechanics, etc.; if they don't care, then I don't care. Have you ever done that yourself? You went into a business and left because you felt like you were intruding. We all have. Although sometimes we have to put up with poor service because we don't have a choice. But

This is what successful people say, do, and when.

then again, often, we do. Sometimes I'd rather go without than give poor service my money.

I know people are sometimes busy and struggle to keep up with client's expectations, but that's why they need training on systems. If they keep ignoring their clients, it won't be long before they are not busy, and it's too late. I have seen this happen many times. I had a terrible customer experience at my local jet ski shop. Coffs City Motors, so I thought I would never go back. I told a friend about it, and they called them Coffs Shitty Motors. About a year later, it closed down. So Shitty habits get shitty results. Better still, good systems create good habits that retain clients.

So when someone takes the time to enter your buying environment, acknowledge those leads ASAP as a priority. Wasn't that the reason why you did everything else? We want people to come to us for their solutions! So if you are busy, do a quick acknowledgement, say something like "Hi, I won't be long". Anything that makes leads feel welcome, regardless of what you sell. When business is good, maybe relaxing on leads is OK, but prioritising leads must be embedded in your muscle memory and business DNA for when it's not. It must be your intentional system and habit.

I am amazed how many people get an enquiry only to react with, "I will call them back tomorrow", not in my world. So we call them up now. I have won many sales by picking up the phone and talking to someone immediately. The reaction I get is fantastic, and they are instantly impressed with how we do business, which makes the sales cycle even faster. Even if I was not the salesperson, I referred the lead to one of the team to follow up with them. In other words, we needed to respond quickly to someone who sent us an inquiry. Then schedule a proper time as required.

Leads are more important than marketing or posting on social media. Handle leads first before you get distracted by other things. Continue your marketing, but don't sacrifice your leads to do marketing!

This is what successful people say, do, and when.

SELL MORE MAKE MORE - The Best Sales Systems Ever!

Have you ever visited Asia and had locals come and try to sell you something just after you arrived? That's because they know that everyone has the same stuff to sell, but we are fresh off the plane, so while we are new and haven't spent all our money, they try to get a sale from us ASAP. They don't let an opportunity go. They don't want us buying the same thing from a vendor down the road. And that's how we need to be with leads too. We can't think they're interested and will say yes, and buy when we are ready. But, no! That's not how it works in sales.

I remember being up after midnight programming in the early days, and an email enquiry came in. I figured he had just emailed me, so I immediately phoned him. He was awake too. He was shocked but also impressed. We laughed at it. We were both awake, so why not? Now you don't have to be as upfront as me, but he did sign up. Maybe it was only because I had responded while he was a hot lead.

Responding quickly to leads builds your positive buying environment. Or in reverse, two, three, and four days later is not a great start. Chances are they are thinking about your competition too, and after two or three days, it may be too late. So if someone wants us now, the sooner they get us, the better. Even if we have to schedule them, do it now!

So it's essential to have a **do-it-now** attitude for leads. You spend so much money and time getting leads into your warm zone, so why let them go? Why wait? They can get sidetracked, buy elsewhere, and spend their money doing something else. They were ready, but we lost them, and it happens to the best of us. But we minimise this by prioritising leads. Even if I have to stop something for a minute and send a quick message to say, "Hey, Tom, I'm just going into a meeting. I will call you back later", most buyers appreciate that and think that's an acceptable acknowledgement, just like a warm welcome from a person in a retail shop or cafe that says "I'll be with you shortly".

Remember, when someone has come into your warm zone, the first action they need is a warm welcome, so give it to them.

This is what successful people say, do, and when.

How Much?

When my wife goes into a dress shop, the first thing she does when a dress catches her eye is look at the price tag. She will instantly decide if it's worth trying on. I do the same thing when I shop, and so do you. And this is why the most common question leads ask is, "How much is it"? We hear that all the time. Don't we? Because we all like to decide on price first. But people buy on value, not price, so how do we handle this question when it's the first thing we are asked?

At ReNet, we consistently received enquiries asking, "Can you email me a price list for a new website"? But this lead is not qualified yet, and their problems are not revealed yet, are they? They have not spoken about their hot spot or where their pain is (CAN Analysis). Sometimes an email would briefly mention a why. But regardless, how can sending prices either fulfil or create a need? It doesn't, and it only answers their price question. But I don't sell on price, and neither should you. You get paid more for selling solutions.

I have trained many people, and most would reply to "How much is it" with something like this if they were ReNet; Website prices start at $1,000 for templates and $5,000 for custom and corporate from $20,000. But what's just happened? They mention price, yet there is no hot spot, pain, or need. So there's got to be a better way!

"But Scotty, they asked for an email with a price list. So I have to do what they say and answer them, don't I"? I get these sorts of questions back to me when I coach people.

Yes, you do, but not as you think.

If you want to sell on price, reply with your best prices. It's not that a price won't work; it does when it's cheap. After all, we shop around all the time based on price tags. But these systems are about increasing your strike rate and making more. So sending a price list is OK if you're ultra-busy, don't care about more business, or want a low-touch sales system. If they do come back, it means they are interested. But if you need to make more sales, then don't!

This is what successful people say, do, and when.

Here's the secret. When a lead asks about pricing, they are asking for more information! So rather than read "How much is it", think of it as them asking, "I don't understand. Can you tell me more about what you do before I make a decision". So whenever someone asks you about pricing, they're asking you for information about why they should buy. Why now, and why from you? And the bigger the price, the more time you spend using your systems to make a deal happen.

Back to how to respond. Let's take a quick look here. What's excellent right now is that someone's reached out as a lead, so you're now in the driver's seat. They haven't purchased from your competition (yet). So the actions you do next will determine their reaction, determining whether you get to the next stage of the cycle. They're now in your warm zone or at least want to get into our warm zone.

So how did we answer these price questions at ReNet? Remember, we can't make a deal from the cold zone, only from our warm zone, meaning some B2B conversation. So our first response was NOT to send an email back but to pick up the phone and talk to them directly ASAP. We would ignore their price question and send me an email request. Here's the thing, the moment we phoned and let them tell us more about what they were looking for, they rarely asked, "How much is it" or "Where's my email"? Why? Because they were now engaged in sharing their why, ONLY then can we offer a value-based solution.

"But Scotty, they asked for an email. Won't they be upset that I didn't send them one"? I was asked this constantly in training too. But no, I can't remember anyone saying, "Why are you phoning? I asked for an email". I can't even remember that happening anyway. The reality is that leads love it when you engage with them. We don't get offended when people help us, nor do they. It's what they want.

Generating Leads

I learnt the power of asking for leads when I was a teenager looking for odd jobs for pocket money. People I did jobs for often referred me to their friends, which was unreal. All I had to do was visit them and

This is what successful people say, do, and when.

mention what I was doing for their friends, and often I got more jobs to do. It was easy to make money. I learnt young always to ask, "Do you know anyone else that might need some work done"? I would ask this regardless of whether they gave me work or not.

OK, asking for referrals is only for some businesses. Like a cafe, asking for a referral every time they served a coffee would be dumb. Then again, if I was starting a cafe, that's how I'd create momentum and encourage any customers I had to bring their friends next time.

In business, people buy leads by advertising and marketing for them, and that's great, but a lead we ask for and get, that's free. So I am amazed at how many people I train that don't ask for referrals!

For example, when I was selling insurance to a mechanic, when I finished the contract and was wrapping up and shaking hands, I knew I hadn't finished yet. I had established know, like, and trust, and they have confidence and belief in the products and me, or they wouldn't have purchased it. So as I'd shake hands, I'd also ask, "Who else do you know that might be interested"? Something like this happened often: "My mate Tom may be interested". I would then get Tom's details and go and see him as soon as possible, if not immediately. Do it now when I get a lead, as they are HOT. These leads are straight into my warm zone because I now have perfect inference.

Sure enough, as I sold ReNet software to real estate agents, I would ask them the same question. Of course, they rarely referred the agent down the road because they compete with each other, but they knew people from different areas, and I used the same system to get free leads from them too.

Often referring people helps build their relationship with other people, as it makes them appear to be looking after each other. Once again, I would contact my free lead as soon as possible. "Hey Tom, I was talking to Paul, and Paul said to give you a call as he believes this will interest you also". See how easy it is to get leads straight into my warm zone? What do you think Tom is going to say? 100% of the time,

Tom would ask me, "What is it"? BOOM! So I'd say, "I'm glad you asked". It's that easy.

I know from coaching sales that most don't dare to ask for leads. Some feel uncomfortable asking the question. But don't feel uncomfortable. Many people love to share leads with their friends. Leads instantly increase your sales without doing any extra work. So get comfortable asking for them.

The funny thing is, I'd ask even when I didn't make a sale. I'm sure people sometimes gave me a few names to get rid of me (LOL). Who cares? Like when I was a teenager, it didn't matter if they purchased. It only mattered that I got a warm lead. And warm leads are free.

Cold Calling Sucks

As a teenager, I cold-called for pocket money. I cold-called for jobs when I left school. In 1990, when I started knocking on the doors of businesses and giving my insurance presentation, it was tough. I still remember my first sale, a half sale ($25) from a guy who had a fishing tackle shop in Harrington, NSW. I couldn't believe someone said "yes" to me after I gave my presentation. I can't remember the second or third sale, but I've never forgotten my first. When I wanted to start IT, I started with website designs. I cold-called selling websites. Then when I began ReNet, yep, I cold-called selling software.

But cold calling sucks, yet I used this system to make money. I have even cold-called a few bookstores to get them to sell my 1st book, the 5 Systems of Successful People, and they are. So cold calling still works today, but experience has taught me the best systems to do it because cold calling sucks.

And if I were starting a business again, I would still drive it. But, rather than build it and hope they'd come, I'd be proactive, make calls and create leads instead. Prospecting and having constructive conversations are among the most effective systems. The good news is that I did make momentum at ReNet, and the last time I made a deliberate cold-calling trip was in September 2003. From then on,

This is what successful people say, do, and when.

SELL MORE MAKE MORE - The Best Sales Systems Ever!

ReNet had enough clients and leads, meaning cold-calling trips were no longer needed. But that took almost four years to make ReNet a company allowing me to focus on the business instead of cold calls.

Now I know you don't want to make cold calls, do you? So don't. Make warm calls instead.

So what's the difference between a cold call and a warm call?

A warm call means having a reason for your call, even if you need to create one. Remember the inference I used to generate pocket money as a teenager? It's precisely the same system in business too.

For example, real estate agents regularly cold-called homeowners to see if they want to sell. So how do they turn a cold call into a warm one? They create a reason. So a house in the same street has been listed for sale or sold is gold, so they knock on the neighbouring doors as a courtesy call to let them know about it. And just like I did, it didn't have to be one they listed or sold. This now means they can do warm calls with some extra knowledge the homeowner may want. See how that has now become a warm call? It's easy to do when we think about it. See how the agent created a warm reason for his call?

Referrals are a great way to create warm calls too. When we approach someone with our opening line of "Tom said come and talk to you," guess what they generally say, "What is it"? I say, "I am glad you asked". I create reasons for my calls, saying something like, "I've come to see you because I've been down the road talking to Tom, and I believe this will interest you also". Or "I've been talking to other local real estate agents". These warm introductions changed the reaction of "Whatever you're selling, I'm not interested" to "What is it"?

Let's do the reverse. Let's say I pick up the phone and want to sell car products to a mechanic. Most people cold call like this. "Hi, Tom, how are you going? I've got some car products you should sell to your customers". But let's change it to a warm lead, "Hey Tom, I was just down the road with John, the mechanic, and he's making extra money from his customers with ABC. I believe they'll interest you also". See how that's a mind-opener for Tom?

This is what successful people say, do, and when.

Can you see how successful people make warm calls? Instead of trying to sell them something cold, they do an introduction with something relevant to them. Something they will want more information on. And that happens to be what we are selling.

The cool thing about this system is that it works even when leads come to us. So we can use the same technique to open people's minds when they ask about our products. As a cafe example, have you ever had the waitress say that something is very popular on the menu? Well, that was them using the same system on us. Although in a cafe, and even though we were already warm, it still worked.

The good news is that you can use the system of warming up leads at every point in your sales system. The better you can turn someone from cold into warm, the better our strike rate is.

Working Your Zones

Have you heard of a 4 4 8? (Sometimes, it's called a 2 2 4).

Our 4 4 8 is how I created leads in my warm and hot zones. Let me explain how it works.

Back in my insurance days, if I sold insurance or had a client in one house or business, what I did then was a 2 2 4. That means I would knock on the two doors to the left, 2 to the right and the 4 across the road. The surrounding places were in my hot zone. So with this system, when I sold someone in one business, I'd immediately go next door to the other businesses and say, "I was just next door with Tom, and I believe this will interest you also". And they'd ask, "What is it"?

That's why I taught this to real estate agents. They could do the same in the real estate industry, a 4 4 8, so they worked their real estate patch and hot spots. That's where they already had some success. So the moment they put up a for sale sign or sell a property, they have a perfect reason for a conversation with the 4 4 8 neighbours.

Success breeds success, and the system here is to prospect the immediate area surrounding where you already have success. The actual

This is what successful people say, do, and when.

SELL MORE MAKE MORE - The Best Sales Systems Ever!

numbers are irrelevant. It can be a 2 2 4 or a 3 3 6. The point is that you are more likely to generate leads in your hot zone. The person next door may not want to buy or sell property, but they might know someone else who does. This is one system I taught real estate agents; those who followed the system sold more properties than those who didn't, and many became million-dollar-a-year writers in sales commissions. Yet it's so simple.

Imagine Tom, the real estate agent, who puts up a for sale sign out the front of a house. Then, he does his 4 4 8, visits the neighbouring homes, and says, "Hi, Mr & Mrs Jones. I am Tom. This is a courtesy call to inform you that the Smiths are selling their house next door, and you may see me here occasionally. I will update you on what is happening so you are informed". Because it's prospecting, Tom has used a warm introduction, and if they were thinking about selling, now is the perfect time for them to ask them, true? And then, when it sells, Tom can do his 4 4 8 again and update all the neighbours on the market, which will generally get a positive response. Can you see how successful real estate agents work their 4 4 8? It's prospecting and building up their database.

Where we've had success, there's a big chance that we will have more success around that. So your 4 4 8 is how you create a hot zone, even if it's a micro-zone.

As another example, what unsuccessful agents do, is ignore their hot zone. Instead, they prospect in their cold zone (where they don't have listings). Others miss the point because all they do is a letter box drop with a brochure or business card in their warm and hot zones. I am sure you have received these too. But seriously, what does a brochure or business card in a letterbox do? Nothing! Yet agents still do this as part of their system because they are scared to talk to B2B with people. I taught real estate agents to take advantage of their hot zones and do warm calls, which took the cold calling fear away for many.

I used this same system when I started building the company ReNet. The first town I visited (outside my local town) was Port Macquarie. It was close to us, and many agents knew each other, so it was nationally in

This is what successful people say, do, and when.

my warm zone. But it was a cold town, and I had to create a hot zone there. Once I did, I kept working in that zone, and then I had to repeat it in the next town, the Gold Coast. So then I also had a hot region. Because of the dense population in QLD, I started focusing only on QLD and gradually spread out my warm and hot zones. Then QLD became my first hot state. And so on. In the end, I had clients all over Australia, but at first, I worked my zones to make this happen.

When I first started, I could have tried any town in Australia, but I knew from experience to be focused on one area and make it hot. Find your hot zones and work on them first. So my 4 4 8 was used in streets, towns, regions and statewide.

Below is a map of where all our client locations across Australia. And having a map like this makes it easy to see where our cold, warm and hot zones are. So if you want more, think about your 4 4 8.

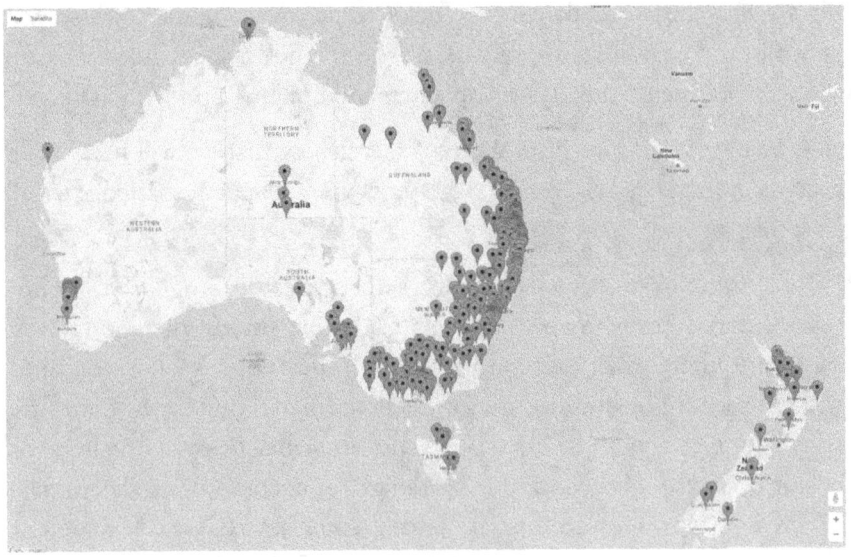

This is what successful people say, do, and when.

Now What?

Win $1,000 worth of free coaching.

Please share a photo with you and a copy of the book on social media, then tag me in it. (Any social media is OK)

And for every 50 entries, someone at random will win, and you stay in the draw for the next random draw. This lasts until 20 draws are won.

Enter the draw by sharing your social media post on the book's webpage my.system1357.com/books (Or follow the QR code below)

Get $1,100 worth of coaching.

Every 50+ copies of this book you order will include a personal one-on-one online training session. So order 50 copies directly with me and give them to your family, friends, clients, or team, and then we are on.

Start Teaching

And start teaching and sharing these systems because once you teach, you are elevated to a new level of understanding, and that is where sales success becomes easier and easier.

Reviews

Sharing your positive book review online would be awesome. It means way more than you think.

So please do a genuine review on amazon.com or comment on the books page my.system1357.com/books; both would be extra awesome!

Vote

Please let me know your favourite system by voting on the book's webpage here my.system1357.com/books.

SELL MORE MAKE MORE - The Best Sales Systems Ever!

Follow

Please follow me on Linkedin and YouTube for more info.

Join

Create an account on System 1357® (www.system1357.com) and watch all videos. It's free to join, the courses cost very little, and there's also a massive amount of free resources. You'll love it.

Thank you!

One day we may cross paths in person at an event I am attending or speaking at, in the surf, or while travelling somewhere. If so, make sure you come and say hi. It would be great to meet you, and that means more than you think.

Thanks again. It's great to be on your team.

Talk soon…

Scotty

This is what successful people say, do, and when.

www.ingramcontent.com/pod-product-compliance
Lightning Source LLC
Chambersburg PA
CBHW051428290426
44109CB00016B/1479